The B-Movie Cookbook!
The 1950s

Fiona Young-Brown

&

Nic Brown

Copyright ©2017 Fiona Young-Brown & Nic Brown all rights reserved.

This book and all content herein is not to be reproduced and/or redistributed in any form, digital, print or other media without the express written permission of Fiona Young-Brown & Nic Brown.

Copyright for the photos included in this book, unless otherwise specifically credited, is the property of Fiona Young-Brown & Nic Brown. Copyright for the original art used for the cover of the book is the property of Fiona Young-Brown & Nic Brown. The film promotional materials used are no longer covered by copyright, to the best of our knowledge. Whilst every effort has been made to trace possible copyright owners, the authors apologize for any omissions and will undertake to make the appropriate changes in subsequent editions of the book.

ISBN: 1546935576
ISBN-13: 978-1546935575

DEDICATION

In memory of Vince Rotolo – Vince, here's one for your collection!

Fiona Young-Brown & Nic Brown

CONTENTS

	Acknowledgments	vii
1	Introduction	9
2	The Thing From Another World	11
3	Creature From the Black Lagoon	22
4	Godzilla	29
5	Them	36
6	Forbidden Planet	42
7	It Conquered the World	50
8	I Was A Teenage Werewolf	57
9	From Hell It Came	62
10	20 Million Miles to Earth	69
11	Special Effects Focus on Ray Harryhausen	76
12	The Blob	80
13	Attack of the 50 Foot Woman	87
14	Revenge of Frankenstein	92
15	Teenagers From Outer Space	98
16	House on Haunted Hill	104
17	Plan 9 From Outer Space	110

ACKNOWLEDGMENTS

As with any book project, there are many more people involved than we will probably remember to thank. However, we will do our best to express our gratitude to all those who have supported and helped us, both directly and indirectly. Huge thanks to Mark Mawston for his assistance with finding images, and to Kelley Baker for continually prodding us. Thanks also to all of the B-Movie Cast listeners who have offered suggestions and encouragement over the past few years.

We'd also like to take this opportunity to thank Vince Rotolo. Vince was the creator of the B-Movie Cast and many of the films we cover in this book were first watched as part of Nic's co-host duties for the show. We love B-Movies, but Vince was a true inspiration for us to look a little deeper at these oft-forgotten film gems. Vince passed away in 2016, but his love of B-Movies lives on in everyone who listens to the show and reads this book.

INTRODUCTION

I'm often asked, "What is a B-Movie?" That's a good question. Film buffs around the world will give you different answers. The generally accepted origin of the term was in reference to the second film of a double-feature from the age when movies often made their rounds in pairs. "A-Movies" (which were rarely referred to that way, strangely enough) were bigger budget and addressed the more serious subject matter. "B-Movies" fell into the lower-budget, less serious gap.

B-Movies really came into their own at the start of the 1950s. Filmmakers like Roger Corman, William Castle, and Bert I. Gordon, grabbed onto the headlines of the day and put out science fiction and horror films like *Attack of the Crab Monsters, The Amazing Colossal Man,* and *The House on Haunted Hill* that played in drive-ins and small-town theaters across the country. The films played to what was on people's minds: the fear of the atomic age, space travel and even ghosts and murder.

"I Was a Teenage…" became a B-Movie calling card as these filmmakers also realized the economic power of a new demographic with free time, transportation and disposable income: teenagers. The rise of the drive-in movie along with the boom in population created a perfect market for low-budget cinema geared towards getting teens in front of screens.

The demand for low-budget filler took another turn with the rise of home video in the 1970s and 80s. Video stores craved more product than Hollywood could make and so the 'direct to video' market was born. Companies like Troma Pictures and Full Moon Video turned out low-budget, fun movies and carried the genre into today's streaming video-on-demand world.

That still doesn't answer the question though of how I define a B-Movie? For that I take a page from my good friend Vince Rotolo. He created the B-Movie Podcast and, over more than 375 episodes, explored what made a B-Movie. The answer: films that had heart and were fun to watch. Movies like *The Blob* or *I Was a Teenage Werewolf* that didn't take themselves too seriously and remembered why eyeballs focus on screens--to be entertained.

My wife, Fiona, and I are both writers. While Fiona has been working in mostly the non-fiction world of history, science and social issues, my writing has tended to go the other way. Werewolves, monsters, magic and guns feature heavily in my books and short stories. So when we decided to do a project together it didn't take us long to find some common ground. Fiona had written a successful history book centered on food, "A Culinary History of Kentucky". The book featured stories about the origins of many traditional Kentucky dishes and cooking styles along with recipes for those same dishes.

I was working with Vince hosting the B-Movie Podcast every week and one of us, I honestly don't remember which, realized that it would be fun for us to blend her love of history and cooking and my love of the B-Movie genre. Thus, "The B-Movie Cookbook" was born.

While the idea of the book was good, actually deciding what films to include was a tough call. We decided to start with what many would consider the 'Golden Age' of the B-Movie-the 1950s. Once we'd narrowed that down, we started picking films. We wanted to include a little bit of everything from the horrors of radiation and atomic science to ghosts and ghouls. We came up with our list and then set about watching the films. I watched them with a critical eye for writing about the movies. Fiona watched them to figure out what connections to food each of them had. Sometimes it was easy. Films like *The Thing from Another World* had so many references to food and eating that it was a struggle to include everything. Other movies like *Forbidden Planet* made us stretch our imaginations a little more.

In the end, we picked fifteen movies and Fiona crafted recipes that fit the theme of each of the films. One thing that is different about this book from other cookbooks though is that we cooked every meal in it. The photos you see are not staged food, although we did try to get creative with the backdrops and settings. We ate every dish that we fixed, usually right after the last picture was taken lest it get too cold. So when you look at the photos remember, that's not just a picture in a cookbook. That was our dinner, dessert or both!

We hope you enjoy the B-Movie themed dishes we've included here. We also hope that you enjoy the films as well. At the end of the day "The B-Movie Cookbook" was a labor of love for me and my wife. We hope that you have as much fun watching these movies and trying these dishes as we had making them.

Bon Appetit!

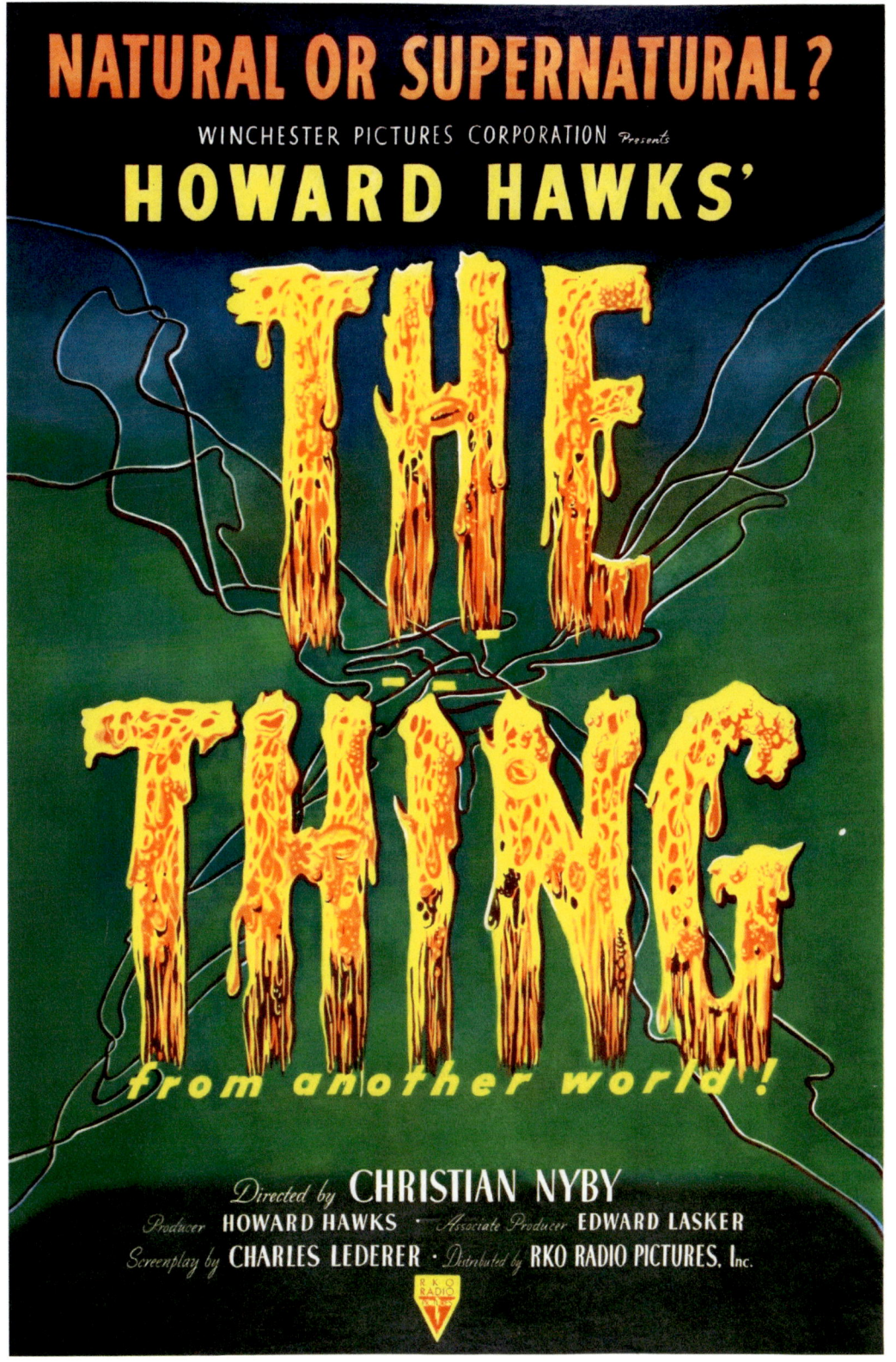

THE THING FROM ANOTHER WORLD

The Thing From Another World (1951)
Directed by Christian Nyby
Written by: Screenplay – Charles Lederer, Original story- John W. Campbell Jr.
Produced by Winchester Pictures Corporation

The Story

> ### Fun Facts
>
> *The film's title is revealed with the letters slowly burning through a black background. Unusual for the day, the title sequence also did not include any of the cast credits. They are shown at the film's end.*
>
> *The film is an adaptation of a novella that appeared in Astounding Science Fiction in 1938 called "Who Goes There" written by John W. Campbell (under the pseudonym Don A. Stuart).*
>
> *The exterior scenes were shot primarily in Glacier National Park. The interior scenes were shot on an LA soundstage built inside an ice house (to allow for the visible breath due to cold seen in the film)*

Captain Hendry (Kenneth Tobey) and his flight crew are dispatched from an American Air Force base in Anchorage, Alaska to a remote scientific station at the North Pole. General Fogerty, their commander, in addition to being obsessed with keeping his office door shut, wants them to investigate a strange craft that the science crew reported crashed in the area. Since he didn't have anything better to do, newspaper reporter and general wise guy, Ned "Scotty" Scott (Douglas Spencer) hitches a ride with the team.

Dr. Carrington (Robert Cornthwaite), leader of the science team, explains that something moving very fast crashed. Photos show that it wasn't a meteor. It's large enough that its metal content throws off magnetic compasses.

The team flies to the scene and finds a ship of unknown origin buried in the ice. They decide to get an idea of its shape by fanning out around it and realize that they have formed a rough circle. Scotty proclaims it's a flying saucer, but since the film's budget didn't include actually showing the ship, the team accidentally blows it up when they try to burn it out of the ice.

Fortunately for the scientists, a creature, possibly the pilot, escaped and was nearby frozen in the ice. They cut out a large block of ice that contains the human-shaped pilot. Unfortunately, the crew learns not to put an electric blanket on the frozen monster you bring back to your base when it wakes up and starts killing the team.

The scientists figure out that the Thing (James Arness in some heavy monster make-up) is a plant-based life form. As such, it's ridiculously hard to kill. It also feeds on blood, so when it plants a little seed garden, it starts draining scientists and flyers to water the plants.

In typical mad scientist fashion, Dr. Carrington decides the creature must live no matter the cost. Not the best idea, perhaps. His secretary, Nikki Nicholson (Margaret Sheridan), stops making goo-goo eyes at Captain Hendry long enough to tell him Carrington is actually using seeds from the Thing to grow his own monster salad mix.

> *Fun Facts*
>
> *The scene where the creature is drenched in kerosene and set on fire is believed to be the first time a full body fire burn was done by a stunt person (Tom Steele).*
>
> *Other than the fire stunt, actor James Arness, played the creature. He was reportedly embarrassed somewhat by the role and called the creature a 'giant carrot'.*
>
> *The scene where the crew spreads out to form the shape of the spacecraft buried in the ice, and form a circle, was actually filmed at the RKO Ranch in the San Fernando Valley in 100-degree heat.*
>
> *There is an urban legend that James Arness, in full "The Thing" make-up, was driving to the studio. He stopped at a red light and apparently scared someone in the car next to him so bad that they passed out.*

After they destroy Carrington's space chia pets, Hendry and some of the less crazy scientists try to figure out a way to kill it. Bullets and fire don't seem to stop the Thing, but Nikki has a better idea. Why not cook it? They break out the electrical gear and set up a trap. Only Carrington has a serious green thumb up his sleeve and they all may end up as plant food if he has his way.

The Food

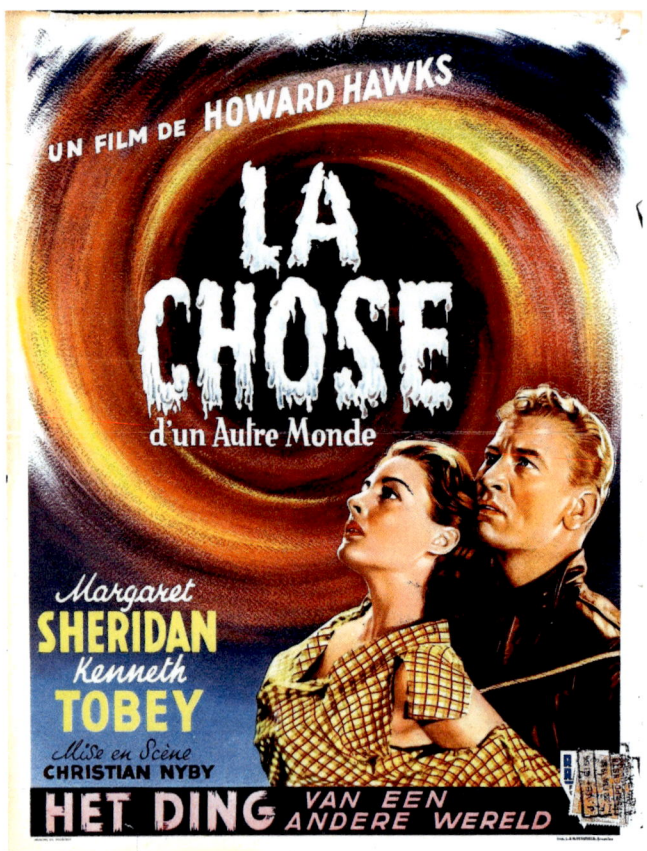

The first movie in the book actually makes a lot of food references and, despite the carrot obsession, most of them are dessert-related. I'm starting to wonder if the movie was sponsored by a coffee company – I don't think ten minutes passes without someone offering coffee. In fact, Nikki's role, other than as love interest, seems to consist entirely of entering rooms and offering the men more hot coffee.

The Thing From Another World's preoccupation with food means there are some great food-related lines in the movie:

"An intellectual carrot. The mind boggles." Scotty to Dr. Carrington.

"I'm not going to accuse you of being full of wild blueberry muffins." Scotty again. I would think that being full of wild blueberry muffins would mean to be happy and content, but apparently, it makes one sort of loony. Who knew!

"Let me take a picture before someone makes a salad of him." Yep, that would also be Scotty; our intrepid journalist gets all the best lines.

However, it is Nikki, while taking a break from pouring coffee, who offers the line that is KEY to them surviving this movie. One of the men asks, "What do you do with a vegetable?"

Nikki's response: "Boil it, stew it, bake it, fry it."

And fry it they do -- with electricity. It just goes to show that without a woman who can cook at the North Pole, we'd all be slaves to the outer space carrot by now!

Salmon with Spicy Roast Carrots and Yogurt

Serves 2

2 salmon steaks
1 lb. / 450g fresh carrots, preferably with some fronds attached
3 tbsp. olive oil
2 tbsp. maple syrup
2 tbs harissa paste
½ cup / 120g plain yogurt
½ tsp grated lemon zest plus extra for garnish
1 tsp fresh dill plus additional for garnish
Salt and pepper

Preheat oven to 230°C/450°F.

Scrub the carrots and cut off most of the fronds. Place in an ovenproof dish.

In a small bowl, mix 2 tbsp. olive oil with the maple syrup and 1 tbsp. of the harissa paste. Drizzle over the carrots and give the dish a shake to make sure they are evenly coated.

Roast the carrots for 35-40 minutes.

Meanwhile, place the salmon steaks in a separate ovenproof dish. Drizzle with the remaining tbsp. of olive oil and season with a little salt and pepper.

When the carrots have about 15 minutes of cooking time left, place the salmon in the oven.

Swirl together the plain yogurt with the lemon zest, remaining harissa, and fresh dill. Don't mix too much; it looks quite attractive to have ribbons of red throughout rather than the mixture turn pink.

Serve the salmon with a spoonful of the spiced yogurt and the spiced carrots. Garnish with a sprinkling of lemon zest and fresh dill.

Scotty's Blueberry Muffins

Makes 12-18 muffins, depending on size of baking liners used

2 cups / 250g plain flour
2 tsp baking powder
½ tsp salt
½ cup / 115g unsalted butter, room temperature
1 cup / 225g sugar
2 eggs
1 tsp vanilla extract
½ tsp almond extract (optional)
½ cup / 120ml milk
2 ½ cups / 150g fresh blueberries
2 tbsp. sugar for sprinkling (optional)

Preheat the oven to 190°C/375°F.

Use paper liners to line a muffin tin or cupcake pan.

Sift together the flour, baking powder, and salt.

In a separate bowl, beat the butter and sugar together for 2-3 minutes until the butter is smooth. Add the eggs and beat well. Lastly, add the vanilla extract, and almond (if using). Stir into the egg mix, making sure to scrape any additional butter from the sides of the bowl.

Continuing with your electric mixer, alternate adding the flour and the milk, combining thoroughly after each addition.

Use a spatula to fold the blueberries into the mix, taking care not to crush them.

Spoon the mix into the lined muffin tin. If you like, you can sprinkle the tops with a little extra sugar.

Bake for 30 minutes until the muffins have risen and are golden brown in color. Remove the pan from the oven and allow to cool for 10 minutes before moving the muffins to a wire rack to cool completely.

Store in an airtight tin.

Deconstructed Baked Alaska
(aka Carrot Cake Meringues with Raspberry Sauce)

What dessert represents the frozen north better than Baked Alaska? But if you're cooking just for two, this smaller deconstructed version is easier and with no leftovers… unless you decide to make seconds.

Serves 2

2 ready-made meringue nests
1 layer carrot cake, cut into rounds (see recipe below)
Vanilla ice cream
1 quantity raspberry sauce (see recipe below)
Fresh raspberries for garnish

Place a round of carrot cake on a plate. Place a meringue nest on top of the cake, the top that with a scoop or two of vanilla ice cream. Drizzle with raspberry sauce and garnish with fresh raspberries.

Carrot Cake

Make this as two layers, and either sandwich together with cream cheese frosting or cut into smaller rounds for the Baked Alaska recipe above.

1 cup / 200g vegetable oil
1 ¼ cups / 275g sugar
3 eggs
1 ½ cups / 80g grated carrots
1 cup / 225g crushed pineapple in juice
1 tsp baking soda
1 tsp cinnamon
½ tsp salt
½ tsp baking powder
2 ¼ cups / 280g plain flour

Preheat oven to 180°C/350°F. Grease 2 8-inch round cake tins.

Mix the oil and sugar until creamy. Beat in the eggs, one at a time, and then add the carrot and pineapple, mixing well.

In a separate bowl, sift the baking soda, cinnamon, salt, baking powder and flour together. Add the flour to the oil and egg mixture, about half a cup at a time, beating until smooth.

Divide the batter between the two greased tins and bake for 25-30 minutes.

Leave the cakes to cool before removing from pans.

Frost or use in the Deconstructed Baked Alaska.

Raspberry Sauce

This makes enough for the Deconstructed Baked Alaska with plenty more for enjoying over ice cream. Leftover sauce can be frozen.

3 cups / 350g raspberries, fresh or thawed from frozen
½ cup / 115g sugar
4 tbsp. water
1 tsp cherry liqueur (optional)

Put the sugar and water in a saucepan and heat gently until the sugar has dissolved. Use a hand blender to puree the raspberries and the sugar syrup. Strain to remove the seeds. Add the liqueur, if using, and stir well. The sauce can be served either cold or warm.

CREATURE FROM THE BLACK LAGOON

The Creature From The Black Lagoon (1954)
Directed by Jack Arnold
Written by Maurice Zimm, Harry Essex, & Arthur A. Ross
Produced by Universal Studios

The Story

While doing some geological research in the Amazon jungle, Dr. Carl Maia (Antonio Moreno) and his team discover a fossilized hand with webbed fingers pointing out of the rocks. Dr. Maia decides to take the hand and visit his old friend and student, Dr. David Reed (Richard Carlson). They figure that this hand could come from a half-man, half-fish missing link. Reed's boss, Dr. Mark Williams (Richard Denning) doesn't see a fossil; he sees dollar signs and agrees to an expedition to look for the rest of the skeleton.

Carl, David, and Mark are joined on the expedition by David's girlfriend and co-worker Kay Lawrence (Julie Adams) as well as Dr. Edwin Thompson (Whit Bissell). The team hires a rough-looking boat named *Rita,* under Captain Lucas (Nestor Paiva) and they head out with a small crew heading for Dr. Maia's expedition's camp.

> *Fun Facts*
>
> *There were two men who played the Gill Man in the film. Ricou Browning played the creature in all of its underwater scenes. Ben Chapman played the creature when it was walking on land.*
>
> *Ricou Browning was a professional diver and swimmer who was in the Gill Man suit during the underwater scenes. Jack Arnold had heard that Browning could hold his breath for up to 5 minutes and wanted him to do so for the film since the suit did not have space for an air tank. Browning did his best but relied on a team of divers with air hoses ready to support him. To let them know he needed air he would simply go limp and they would bring the hose to him.*

Unfortunately for Dr. Maia, and more so for his team at the camp, there are more than just fossilized hands in that part of the jungle. While Carl was away showing off his bones, the amphibious Gill Man decided to pay the camp a visit. Being good scientists, the crew got scared and attacked the curious creature. Having been attacked, Gill Man did what Gill Man does; it killed Dr. Maia's whole team. So when the new crew arrives, they find the camp wrecked and everyone dead.

Not to be deterred by finding a whole camp of researchers slaughtered, Dr. Reed and the others

> ### *Fun Facts*
>
> *The director Arnold believed that the Gill Man wouldn't emit bubbles so the suit couldn't either. That's why there was no room made for an air tank. Later films would ignore the idea and the suits were built to hold air tanks. The subsequent bubbles were ignored.*
>
> *There were two styles of Gill Man suits -- a darker one for when the creature was out of the water and a lighter one to make it easier to see when it was in the water. The water suit was not just a lighter color; it was also lighter in weight to make it easier for Browning to swim in.*
>
> *Aside from the film's two sequels Revenge of the Creature and The Creature Walks Among Us, the Gill Man made a number of other appearances in film and television. It was seen as "Uncle Gilbert" in an episode of the television show The Munsters. An updated version of the Gill Man appeared as one of the classic horror monsters that invade a small town in Monster Squad. Gill Man was also reborn as a CGI animated monster in Monsters vs Aliens.*

continue the expedition. They have very little luck at turning up more bones, but their stay gives the Gill Man plenty of time to check out Kay. Although interspecies romance seldom turns out well, the Gill Man decides to stalk Kay. He follows the team further up river in search of the "Black Lagoon" where they believe the rest of the skeleton may have ended up.

Once there, Kay decides that the Black Lagoon in the middle of the Amazon is the perfect place to go for a swim and she dives right in. Gill Man is kind of pleased by this and spends a lot of time swimming right under her and generally being a creeper without ever actually touching her. He isn't so lucky when he gets caught up in a drag line and loses a claw. The scientists are excited to find evidence that there is an actual creature alive and in the lagoon with them.

Captain Lucas's crew loses some of their enthusiasm when the creature starts taking them out in an attempt to score some quality time with Kay. But the creature slips up and the team captures him. They lock him up on the ship and leave Dr. Thompson to keep watch. Thompson has been hitting the sauce, and we don't mean tartar, so he ends up letting the creature escape.

Mark is still seeing dollar signs and wants the Gill Man captured, but agrees they need to leave and come back better prepared. Gill Man has other ideas. He blocks the mouth of the lagoon so he can take another shot at Kay. She plays hard to get, but at least the creature does the scientific community a favor and mauls Mark to death. Then he takes Kay back to his cave for some sushi. David and the guys show up and spoil the mood by filling the Gill Man full of lead. The film ends with poor Gill Man sinking into the lagoon.

The Food

Although on the surface one might not find many, or indeed any, food clues in Creature from the Black Lagoon, we don't have to look too far to find some inspiration. We've created our own black lagoon in the form of a risotto colored with squid ink. And for our monstrous creature, we used snow crab claws, although grilled octopus tentacles would be equally at home. For dessert, it seemed appropriate to choose a dish from South America; fudgy brigadeiros truffles fit the bill.

Squid Ink Risotto

Serves 4

2 tbsp. olive oil
1 shallot, chopped finely
2 garlic cloves, chopped finely
1 cup / 200g Arborio rice
⅓ cup / 75ml dry white wine
2 tsp squid ink
3 cups / 750ml fish stock, warmed
1 tbsp. butter (optional)
salt and pepper

lemon wedges

Heat the olive oil in a large saucepan over a medium-high heat. Add to the pan the shallot and garlic. Cook for one minute.
Add the rice to the pan and stir to coat with oil. Pour the wine over the rice and allow to reduce to half its volume.

At this point, stir in a teaspoon of the squid ink and 1 cup of the fish stock. Reduce the heat to medium. Cook until almost all of the liquid has been absorbed and then add more stock. Continue to cook in this manner, adding stock when the previous amount has been mostly absorbed. When the rice is cooked and most of the liquid has been absorbed, stir in the remaining teaspoon of squid ink, as well as salt and pepper to taste. The butter may also be added at this point to add to the creaminess of the risotto.

Serve bowls of the risotto, topped with steamed crab claws, grilled calamari mix or your favorite "sea monster" and some lemon wedges.

Brigadeiros

1 14oz can sweetened condensed milk
3 tbsp. cocoa powder
1 tbsp. unsalted butter, room temperature
1 tsp vanilla extract
Extra butter for rolling
Sprinkles

Whisk the condensed milk and cocoa powder together in a saucepan until the mixture is smooth, with no lumps. Add the butter. Cook over a medium heat for about 10 minutes. Stir constantly and lower the heat if necessary to prevent scorching. The mixture should thicken up into a light fudge consistency. Stir in the vanilla extract, remove from heat, and leave until it is cool enough to touch.

When the mixture has cooled, roll it into small balls. Since it can be sticky, a little softened butter on your hands can help with the process. Then roll each ball in sprinkles. Chill for an hour before eating.

GODZILLA: KING OF THE MONSTERS

Godzilla, King of the Monsters (1956) [Chapter Head]
Directed by Ishiro Honda (Original Japanese) and Terry Morse (American version)
Written by Ishiro Honda, Takeo Murata and Al C. Ward
Produced by Toho Company (Original Japanese) and Jewell Enterprises, Inc.

The Story

> ### Fun Facts
>
> *The film was a modified version of director Ishiro Honda's 1954 film "Godzilla". Jewell Enterprises, Inc. acquired the international rights to the film in 1955. They decided to rework the film for a Western audience by adding the character of Steve Martin (Raymond Burr), an American reporter. Through editing and the use of doubles for the original cast (only seen from behind or obscured in some way), American director Terry O. Morse created the sense that Burr was there, interacting with the characters in the original film.*
>
> *The reworked film cut much of the original's anti-atomic weapons references, only briefly identifying the probable cause of the creature's awakening as being nuclear testing in the South Pacific.*

Ships have been mysteriously disappearing from the waters around Odo Island off the coast of Japan. The Japanese government is baffled by the problem. Even more baffling is why the Japanese keep letting American Steve Martin (Canadian actor Raymond Burr) go wherever he wants while covering the story.

Martin, with the help of a Japanese Security Forces liaison named Tomo Iwanaga (Frank Iwanaga), heads to Odo Island after a survivor is found. They hear the survivor talk of a giant monster attacking his ship and learn that the locals have a legend of a "God of Sea Monster" they call Gojira. To make sure Martin understands what they said, Iwanaga immediately and spectacularly mispronounces the name and calls the monster Godzilla and thus a legend is born.

Martin meets up with Dr. Yamane, the scientist leading the investigation. They discover giant radioactive footprints on the island. Then an alarm sounds and the whole village runs for hills as Godzilla appears! Yamane is convinced Godzilla was a dormant dinosaur of some kind that was awakened by nuclear testing. No one seems to care about the nuclear link though; they just want to destroy the monster.

In a strange twist of amazing plot convenience, Martin is friends with another scientist named Dr. Serizawa. Serizawa is betrothed to Yamane's daughter Emiko in an arranged marriage, but Emiko doesn't love him. She loves Ogata, a salvage ship captain. When she goes to tell Serizawa the wedding is off, he shows her his new invention: the Oxygen Destroyer. This is a terrible weapon and Emiko is so stunned by its power that she forgets to break off the engagement.

Meanwhile, Godzilla has been thinking he'd like to spend a little quality time in Tokyo. So he pops out of the water and starts running amok in the town before calling it a night. The Japanese figure he'll be back and set up a trap with high voltage wires. That just makes Godzilla angry and he proceeds to devastate Tokyo.

Martin, who for some reason can't seem to be in the same spot as any of the Japanese he's working with, reports on the attacks and is almost killed. Emiko comes to see him in the hospital and tells him about his buddy Serizawa's weapon of mass destruction and his plan to never, ever use it. They decide Serizawa needs to be convinced otherwise.

Emiko goes back to see Serizawa and she takes her true love Ogata with her. It makes sense, if you want to get your fiancé to hand over a weapon, you should take the guy you really love to talk to him about it. Serizawa resists until he sees footage of Godzilla's destruction. Shocked by the devastation, he agrees to set up the Oxygen Destroyer in Tokyo Bay to take out the monster.

> ## Fun Facts
>
> *1977 Italian filmmaker Luigi Cozzi bought the rights to the film for the Italian market and used an early form of colorization called "Spectorama 70" on the film so Italian distributors would release the film. Nicknamed "Cozzilla".*
>
> *Raymond Burr spent six days on set working on the film, though an urban myth had him on set for only one day.*
>
> *Writer Al C. Ward, who was responsible for scripting the American version, was reportedly offered $2500 or 5% of the film's profits for his work. Believing the film would not do well, Ward took the up-front cash. Based on the film's success, his 5% profit share would have been worth millions.*
>
> *The original film received a nomination for the Japanese version of the Academy Award for Best Picture of 1954. It lost to Akira Kurosawa's "The Seven Samurai". However, it did win an award for Best Special Effects.*
>
> *In the original Japanese version, Godzilla was described as being about 150 feet tall. In the American version, he was said to be about 400 feet tall. The reason for the change was concern that the monster would seem too small in a setting like New York where buildings were not restricted in height by concerns for earthquake safety.*

Martin somehow again finds himself at the center of the action, or at least slightly to the left and off camera of it, when he's on the boat that takes Serizawa, Ogata, and Emiko to the spot where Godzilla's sleeping under the ocean. Ogata and Serizawa dive in and plant the device. Then Serizawa cuts his own airline, sends Ogata to the surface and detonates the Oxygen Destroyer. He figures it's best that he dies with his invention rather than seeing it fall into the wrong hands. Godzilla and every other living thing in Tokyo Bay melt. Meanwhile, Ogata and Emiko are now free to go off and lead a life of romantic fulfillment. For his part, Martin never does quite enter the camera frame with any of the other main characters, but he's still back for a follow-up movie in 1985.

The Food

The obvious choice here is a selection of sushi rolls. Making them is not as difficult as might first seem, and once rolling them has been mastered, you can chop and change the fillings to match your own tastes.

But… that's not quite enough. After all, one of these things is not like the others.

You can't deny the awkwardness of Steve Martin being sandwiched into the American remake, so it seems only right to make one roll that doesn't quite match. Our Raymond Burr roll represents the all-American Steve with canned sausages, processed cheese, and yellow mustard.

It's surprisingly good.

Sushi Rice

2 ½ cups / 500g short-grain sushi rice
2 ½ cups / 625 ml water
2-inch strip of kombu (optional)
4 tbsp. rice vinegar
2 tbsp. sugar
2 tsp salt
2 tbsp. mirin or sherry (optional)

If you are using a rice cooker, follow the device's instructions.
Rinse the rice in cold water and leave to drain for 30 minutes. Put in a pan with the 2½ cups of water and the strip of kombu if you have some. Bring to the boil. When the water comes to a boil, put the lid on the pan and turn the heat down to low. Do not lift the lid but leave the rice on low for 15 minutes. Remove from the heat but do not remove the lid for another 10 minutes. Meanwhile, mix together the rice vinegar, sugar, salt, and mirin, making sure the sugar dissolves. Remove the kombu strip.

Put the rice into a large bowl and pour the vinegar mixture over the rice. Mix to ensure that the rice is thoroughly coated with the liquid. The mixing will also help to cool the rice.

Cover the rice with a damp towel until it is cooled to room temperature and you are ready to use it. This will prevent the rice from drying out

Sushi rolls

1 quantity of sushi rice
Nori sheets
Fillings of your choice. We used:
Cucumber, sliced into strips
Artificial crab meat
Cream cheese
Sushi-grade tuna, sliced or finely diced and mixed with mayonnaise and sriracha
Avocado
Finely chopped spring onion
Mayonnaise
Sriracha

Raymond Burr Roll

Sushi rice
Nori sheets
Canned Vienna sausages
Slices of processed cheese
Yellow mustard

Making sushi rolls is not as complicated as it might seem, if you have the right tools and ingredients. In addition to sushi-quality fish and the proper rice, you also need a sharp knife. A bamboo mat makes rolling much easier, although you can get by with plastic wrap if needed.

To make a basic roll with nori on the outside:
Place a sheet of nori on your bamboo mat. Spread a layer of rice across the nori, leaving about 1cm clear at the top. Add your selected fillings. Roll carefully and tightly, squeezing together to ensure a good fit. Cut into 6 or 8 rounds.

To make an inside-out roll:

Place a sheet of nori on your bamboo mat. Spread a layer of rice completely across the sheet. Use a little pressure to make sure the rice sticks well. Turn the rice-covered nori over so that the rice is face down. Add your fillings, and roll as before. Cut into rounds.

THEM

Them (1954)[
Directed by Gordon Douglas
Written by Ted Sherdeman and Russell Hughes (Screenplay) George Worthing Yates (Original Story)
Produced by Warner Bros. Pictures

The Story

Two state troopers, Ben Peterson (James Whitmore) and Ed Blackburn (Chris Drake), patrolling the highways of the New Mexico desert find a little girl wandering in a state of shock. They search for her family and find their camper trailer; it has been partially destroyed and the family is gone. The only clues are an odd footprint in the sand and a strange, pulsing tone that is heard briefly.

Later Gramps, the owner of the most poorly located general store in the south-west, is found dead. His store is wrecked and all the sugar is gone. Trooper Peterson leaves Trooper Blackburn in the store while he goes to file a report. Bad move as the crazy pulsing noise is back and when Blackburn goes to investigate, he is attacked and killed.

Now the FBI is interested enough to send an agent to look into the strange goings on. They send Special Agent Robert Graham (James Arness). Graham brings along a couple of entomologists, Dr. Harold Medford (Edmund Gwenn) and his daughter, Dr. Pat Medford (Joan Weldon). You'd think that the agent and the trooper would have figured out something strange was going on when the government sends insect specialists to investigate deaths, but that might be asking too much.

So the mixed team, in an amazing demonstration of government agency cooperation, begin to search for the truth.

What do they find?

> *Fun Facts*
>
> *Walt Disney watched the film while considering James Arness for the role of Davey Crocket in his Disneyland TV Show. He saw Fess Parker (who had a small, but memorable role in the film) and liked his work so much he cast him.*
>
> *The film was originally supposed to be shot in color and in 3D. However, just before production started, the studio scrapped the color and 3D filming plans in favor of the cheaper black and white option. They kept the red and blue opening title shot to give the movie some punch.*
>
> *John Wayne watched the film and liked James Arness's performance so much that he recommended him for the role of Marshal Matt Dillon in the TV show Gunsmoke. Arness got the role and played that character from 1956 to 1976.*

> **Fun Facts**
>
> *The "Wilhelm scream", a stock sound effect of a man screaming, is used three times in Them. The same scream has been used over 200 times in movies and television including in the Star Wars and Indiana Jones films.*

Giant ants. The ants are believed to be the result of nuclear weapon testing in the area. Dr. Medford tells them how best to destroy the giant ants using poison gas and bazookas, but a pair of young queens that still have their wings manage to fly away and escape.

Now it's a race against the biological clock as the FBI, the army, two entomologists and one New Mexico state trooper try to find the queens. They follow leads of UFO sightings and sugar thefts and soon find themselves in the storm sewers under Los Angeles. But they have to do it quickly before the ants can do what mommy ants and daddy ants do when they love each other very much... create a colony of super-sized ants that will eventually destroy all human life on the planet.

The Food

Ants.

Don't worry, we're not about to give you a series of insect-made dishes, although the little critters are the inspiration.

Our main dish is a Chinese offering, so-called because it resembles a group of tiny ants climbing along the branches of a tree (the noodles). Use your imagination!

Since ants are the bane of any summer picnic, dessert is a sugary cake, with lots of frosting. Plastic ants are an optional extra.

Ants in a Tree

Serves 2

2 portions of vermicelli or rice noodles
1 cup / 225g minced pork
Pinch salt
1 tbsp. sesame oil
1 tbsp. tobanjan or similar chili paste
1 tbsp. soy sauce
1 spring onion, diced finely but white and green separated
2 cloves garlic, minced
1 tsp fresh ginger, grated
1 cup / 250ml chicken stock

Soak the noodles in warm water for about 10 minutes. Drain.

Heat the oil in a wok or skillet. Sprinkle the salt over the ground pork and fry until browned. Move the pork to a plate. Add the tobanjan, garlic, ginger, and white part of the spring onion to the pan, Stir fry for 2 minutes. Return the pork to the pan and add the soy sauce, stirring everything together.

Add the stock and bring to a boil. Lastly, add the noodles and stir well. Cook off most but not all of the liquid before transferring to bowls. Sprinkle with the green onion before serving.

Layered Buttercream Cake

4 ½ cups / 550g all-purpose flour

4 tsp baking powder

½ tsp salt

1 ½ cups / 340g unsalted butter, room temperature

2 ¼ cups / 500g sugar

6 eggs, room temperature

2 tsp vanilla extract

2 ¼ cups / 525 ml milk, room temperature

Food color of your choice
Vanilla buttercream (see below)

Preheat oven to 170°C/325°F. Grease 3 or 4 round cake tins. Line the bottoms of the tins with parchment paper and grease that.
Sift together the flour, baking powder, and salt.
Beat the butter and sugar with an electric mixer until fluffy. Add in the eggs, one at a time, and beat until each is thoroughly mixed in. Add the vanilla.
Alternate adding the flour and milk, mixing after each addition.

Divide your cake mix between 3 or 4 bowls (depending how many layers you are making). Add food coloring to each bowl. Liquid food coloring is easier since you can control how many drops you add. You might want to add, for example, 3 drops to one bowl, 5 to another, and so on. Make them all different shades or all the same.

Pour the colored batters into the cake tins. Bake for 25-35 minutes. If using 4 tins, you will need the lesser cooking time, more if using 3 tins. The layers are done when a toothpick comes out clean.

Move the tins to a wire rack and cool for 10 minutes. Then turn over onto the rack to cool completely and easy removal from the tins.

Sandwich together with thick layers of vanilla buttercream (see below) or your favorite frosting.

Vanilla Buttercream

2 lb. / 900g powder sugar
2 cups / 450g unsalted butter, room temperature
¼ cup / 60 ml whipping cream
1 tbsp. vanilla extract

With an electric mixer, beat the butter until soft and smooth. Slowly add the sugar, and beat well. Lastly, add the cream and vanilla. Mix until buttercream is fluffy.

FORBIDDEN PLANET

Forbidden Planet (1956)
Directed by Fred M. Wilcox
Written by Cyril Hume (Screenplay) Irving Block and Allen Adler (Original Story)
Produced by Metro-Goldwyn-Mayer

The Story

In the 23rd century, Earth ship C-57D has been sent to Altair IV to investigate the disappearance of an expedition sent to the planet 20 years earlier. Dr. Morbius (Walter Pidgeon) radios from the surface. He warns that it's too dangerous to land and tells them the survivors don't need any help. Commander Adams (Leslie Nielsen) insists, so Morbius relents and the ship touches down near the Doctor's home.

Morbius sends Robby the Robot to get Adams, Lt. Freeman (Jack Kelly), and Ship's Doctor "Doc" Ostrow (Warren Stevens). They arrive at Morbius's home where they meet the doctor and his daughter, Altaira (Anne Francis).

Dr. Morbius explains that the entire crew of the Bellerophon was killed off by a strange "planetary force". Only he and his wife were spared. Just after Altaira was born, Mrs. Morbius died of natural causes. While Dr. Morbius has spent the last 20 years studying the alien technology of the planet, Altaira has been growing up alone. So when she meets the all-male crew of C-57D, she goes a little boy crazy, much to the annoyance of Morbius.

> *Fun Facts*
>
> *he film has a number of science fiction film firsts. It was the first movie to show humans traveling faster than light speed in a ship that they built. It was also the first film to be set entirely on another planet or in space.*
>
> *Anne Francis's miniskirt was the first worn in a Hollywood movie.*
>
> *The same milestone miniskirt got the film banned by Spanish censors who thought it was a bit too short. It remained banned from Spain until 1967.*
>
> *The film was shot entirely indoors on sound stages at MGM's Culver City Studio, taking up about 89,000 square feet of space.*
>
> *The garden at Morbius's home is actually part of the munchkin village set from "The Wizard of OZ".*

Suddenly that invisible "planetary force" starts stomping around, sabotaging the Earth ship's equipment and killing some of the crew.

Morbius reveals the secret of Altair IV. It used to be the home of the Krell, a super-advanced race that developed the ability to generate matter with their minds. Their society was destroyed seemingly overnight by an unknown force. Morbius has spent the last 20 years studying their technology, even going so far as taking a brain boost from one of the Krell teaching machines. Now Morbius is the keeper of their technology and he's getting really annoyed by the other Earthmen.

When Morbius is annoyed, bad things happen. While the doctor is napping, an invisible monster attacks the ship. None of the ship's weapons can stop it and it looks like everyone will be killed, if not for that fact that Morbius wakes up and the monster vanishes.

Just to make sure Morbius is really pissed off, Altaira and Adams also reveal that they are madly in love. (Barely know her? Feh, who cares?) Adams goes to confront Morbius. He figures out that it's Morbius's subconscious mind using the Krell machines to generate the killer monster.

It's going to kill Adams and maybe Altaira too. Morbius knows he must sacrifice himself. Before he dies, he tells the Commander how to blow up the planet (which is shockingly easy, put a warning label on that switch or something). Adams takes Altaira and Robby and they all scoot before the planet blows its top.

> ## *Fun Facts*
>
> *Props from the film, including the spaceship, the uniforms and some of the ground vehicles, were used repeatedly in other productions, most notably numerous episodes of "The Twilight Zone".*
>
> *Robert Kinoshita was the main designer and builder of Robby the Robot. He was later the art designer for the TV show "Lost in Space" and he cites his work on "Forbidden Planet" as having influenced his design of "the Robot" on the show as well as the Jupiter 2 space craft's saucer shape.*
>
> *The story is often compared to Shakespeare's "The Tempest" for some of the plot points and its isolated location.*
>
> *Robby the Robot was built specifically for the film at a cost of over $100,000 (a large sum for a single movie prop when the film was made). He later appeared in "The Invisible Boy" and several sci-fi TV shows including two episodes of "Lost in Space".*

The Food

Let's face it – this movie is all about the id and one's deepest desires. So the menu is all about decadently rich desserts, with a good measure of booze in honor of cook.

Chocolate Irish Cream Cheesecake

1 cup / 85g graham cracker crumbs
¼ cup / 50g butter, room temperature
2 tbsp. sugar
1 tsp unsweetened cocoa powder
3 (225g) packages cream cheese, softened
1 cup / 225g sugar
3 eggs
½ lb. / 225g semisweet chocolate chips
2 tbsp. heavy cream
1 cup / 225g sour cream
½ cup / 115ml Irish cream liqueur
Fresh whipped cream and raspberries for decoration

Preheat oven to 180°C/350°F. Lightly grease a 9-inch spring form pan with butter.
Combine the crumbs, butter, 2 tbsp. sugar, and cocoa in a small bowl. When mixed well, press into the bottom of the prepared spring form pan.

Place the cream cheese in a large bowl and beat with an electric mixer set to low speed until smooth. While beating, slowly add 1 cup sugar and then the eggs, one at a time. Continue beating until smooth.

Combine the chocolate chips and cream in a microwave-safe bowl. Heat in the microwave until the chocolate is completely melted, stirring every 30 seconds. Beat the chocolate into the cream cheese mixture. Add the sour cream and liqueur, and blend until smooth. Pour the mixture over the crust. Place the pan into a large, deep baking dish. Fill the dish with water to cover the bottom half of the spring form pan.

Bake the cheesecake in the water bath in the preheated oven for 45 minutes; turn oven off; leave the cheesecake in the oven with oven door slightly ajar another 45 minutes; remove from oven. Run a knife along the edge of the cheesecake to loosen from pan. Chill in refrigerator at least 4 hours.

Decorate with cream and fresh raspberries before serving.

Bourbon Nut Brownies

1 ¼ cups / 200g semi-sweet chocolate chips
½ cup / 125g butter
2 eggs
2/3 cup / 150g light soft brown sugar
½ cup / 115g sugar
1/3 cup / 75ml bourbon
1 ½ cups / 175g all-purpose flour
1 cup / 125g pecans or walnuts, chopped

Preheat the oven to 170°C/325°F. Grease an 8-inch square pan, or line with foil.
Put the chocolate chips and butter in a microwave-safe bowl. Heat for 30-second periods, stirring in between, until the chocolate chips have melted.
Whisk the brown and white sugars into the eggs until the sugar dissolves. Stir in the melted chocolate and butter mix, followed by the bourbon. Beat in the flour, and finally, add the chopped nuts.
Pour into the cake tin and bake for 25 minutes, until a toothpick, when inserted, comes out nearly but not completely clean.

Choco-Rum Mousse

Serves 2

1 tbsp. cocoa powder
2 ½ tbsp. boiling water
½ cup / 90g semi-sweet chocolate chips
¾ cup / 180 ml whipping cream
2 tsp sugar
1 tsp rum
Cream and cherries for topping

Dissolve the cocoa powder in the water.
Melt the chocolate chips in the microwave, stirring after each 30-second interval. Mix the dissolved cocoa powder into the melted chocolate.

Using an electric mixer, beat the cream and sugar until the cream has thickened into soft peaks.
Stir the melted chocolate and the rum into the cream.
Pour into serving glasses and chill for at least 2 hours.
Top with whipped cream and cherries before serving.

IT CONQUERED THE WORLD

It Conquered the World (1956)
Directed by Roger Corman
Written by Lou Rusoff and Charles B. Griffith
Produced by Roger Corman and American International Pictures

The Story

Dr. Tom Anderson (Lee Van Cleef) thinks he's doing our troubled Earth a favor when he decides to help an upside-down ice cream cone from Venus take over the world. The creature really wants to enslave mankind, but Anderson thinks it's just going to help by eliminating those pesky emotions that are always getting humans in trouble.

Like any advance alien invader would, the creature moves into a little cave in the hills from which it can launch its attack. Using its advanced technology the invader shuts down all power sources in the world (except for Anderson's house and car). Millions probably died during that mess, but the film couldn't afford to show that. Instead, we follow Dr. Nelson (Peter Graves) as he tries to convince Anderson this is a bad idea.

Meanwhile, the creature sends out mind-control devices that look like a pancake/bat mash-up. They take control of key people, making them emotionless slaves to the alien. There is even one for Nelson, but he manages to escapes his. Unfortunately, his wife Joan (Sally Fraser) doesn't. Rather than restraining her and seeing if there is a way to free her mind of the alien's control, Nelson takes the easy route and shoots her.

> ### Fun Facts
>
> The 'Creature' was designed to be short and squat because director Roger Corman believed that Venus had higher gravity than Earth, and so it would be low to the ground. He later admitted it should've been bigger. They added a 'top' to it that tapers to a point to make the monster taller than Beverly Garland.
>
> When leading lady Beverly Garland got her first look at the titular monster, her sarcastic remark was, "THAT conquered the world?"
>
> Special effects man Paul Blaisdell designed, built, and played the creature. Blaisdell named it Beulah, The cast and crew gave it their own names including Tee-Pee Terror, the Cucumber Critter, and the Carrot Monster.

> **Fun Facts**
>
> *Reportedly the film was shot in just 5 days.*
>
> *In 1966 the film was remade almost shot-for-shot by Larry Buchanan. Buchanan got the rights to a number of American International Pictures films and re-shot them on 16mm film, but in color for sale to the growing television market that wanted more programing in color.*

Anderson's wife Claire (Beverly Garland) may be enjoying being one of the only people on the planet who can still take a hot shower, but she is upset by all the death and violence. In the name of peace she decides to go kick the upside-down ice cream cone alien's ass. The millions of deaths and world-wide chaos and destruction he's helped unleash through his new BFF may not concern Anderson, but when Claire is in danger he decides to act. He teams up with Nelson, who really steps it up and blows off losing his own wife to save Claire. They team up with a random troop of Army men who were on maneuvers in the area. Together they head for the creature's secret cave in hopes of saving Claire and turning the lights back on. Hopefully, someone brought a flamethrower and some salad dressing, because the horror of an evil cucumber alien may be unstoppable.

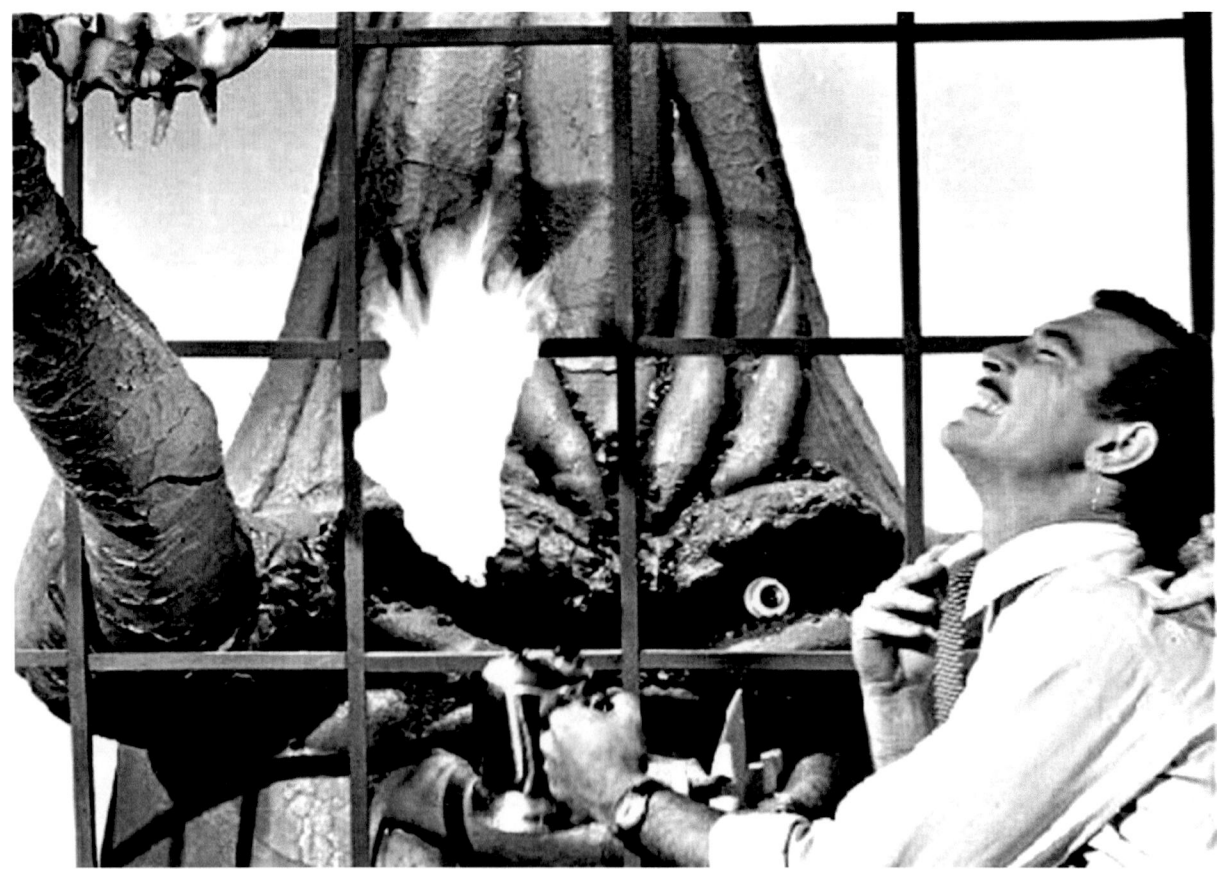

The Food

That monster… it seems no one could quite decide what it was or what it was supposed to be. According to some, the monster, nicknamed Beulah, was supposed to be a fungus, hence a dish of fresh mushrooms in garlic.

At the same time, Frank Zappa paid tribute to the monster in a song on his album Roxy & Elsewhere (1973). He described Beulah as an "inverted ice-cream cone head with fangs". This reminded me of the marshmallow and coconut ice-cream cones I enjoyed as a child. Add some red dye, since the model was, in fact, a beet-red color.

Garlic Sautéed Mushrooms

Serves 2

3 cups / 225g fresh mushrooms, I used a combination of oyster and shiitake
2 tbsp. butter
2 cloves garlic, finely chopped
Black pepper

If using shiitake, button, or larger mushrooms, slice them before cooking. I like to keep the oysters whole because they are so pretty.

Melt the butter over a medium heat and cook the garlic for 1 minute. Add the mushrooms the skillet and sauté for 5-8 minutes. Take care not to break the mushrooms up by stirring too much. Season with freshly ground black pepper and serve on a bed of pasta or zucchini noodles, with yogurt dill sauce on the side.

Yogurt Dill Sauce

This pairs well with the sautéed mushrooms or with fish.
Makes 1 cup

1 cup / 245g plain yogurt
1 clove garlic, minced
1 tbsp. fresh chopped dill
Salt and pepper

Combine all of the ingredients, adding salt and pepper to taste. A few chili flakes or a little lemon juice can also be added if preferred.

Marshmallow Cones

Ice cream cone cups
Chocolate syrup
Marshmallow fluff
Flaked coconut
Red food coloring

Mix a few drops of red food coloring into the coconut and put to one side.

Spoon some marshmallow fluff deep into each ice cream cup. Now squirt 1-2 spoonfuls of chocolate syrup. Top off with more marshmallow fluff, shaping into a rounded dome. Sprinkle with the colored coconut.

I WAS A TEENAGE WEREWOLF

I Was A Teenage Werewolf (1957)
Directed by Gene Fowler Jr.
Written by Herman Cohen and Aben Kandel
Produced by American International Pictures

The Story

Tony Rivers (Michael Landon) is a troubled teen. He's got a hot temper and resorts to violence at the drop of a hat. He's also got a great head of hair, but that isn't going to help him when he accidentally punches his best gal Arlene (Yvonne Lime) in the face when she tries to break up a fight! Whoops!

Tony knows he's got problems so he decides to do what every troubled teen in the 1950s would do: put his trust in science! He goes to see Dr. Brandon (Whit Bissell), a psychologist who works for the local aircraft plant… yes, aircraft plants had psychologists; now let's move on.

Dr. Brandon seems to be helping Tony, but really he's just using the teen as a guinea pig to test a new scopolamine serum he's been developing. Brandon thinks by sending humans back to their most primitive state, using hypnosis and his new drug, he can somehow save mankind from nuclear destruction. Sounds a little crazy? Well, remember this is the same era when doctors sold cigarettes on TV.

Tony does seem to be doing better. At least until he reverts to his 'primitive' state after a party. Among other things, Dr. Brandon proves Darwin had it wrong. Apparently apes had nothing to do with ancient man since Tony's primitive state is that of a werewolf with a serious overbite. Now our teenage werewolf is on the loose in the woods where he comes across the world's only 40-year-old teenager, Frank (Michael Rogas).

Fun Facts

This was the first film to use the "I Was a Teenage…" in its title.

One of American International Pictures' most successful films, it grossed over $2,000,000 on a budget of less than $100,000.

It was released as a double feature with "Invasion of the Saucer Men"

The murdered gymnast, Theresa, was played by 1957 Playboy playmate Dawn Richards whose pictorial hit newsstands just a few months ahead of the movie's release.

It was the first of four teenage monster films to be released by AIP: "I Was a Teenage Frankenstein", "Blood of Dracula" and "How to Make a Monster"

Michael Landon (the Teenage Werewolf himself) revisited the character, in a manner of speaking, in a 1987 episode of the TV show Highway to Heaven entitled "I Was a Middle-Aged Werewolf".

Frank made that classic movie mistake of taking a shortcut through the woods and ends up being puppy chow for Tony.

The police are baffled by the horrific murder in the woods and try to blame it on wild dogs or some other animal. Beat officer Chris Stanley (Guy Williams) doesn't think the detective's theory fits though. He discusses the classified details of the case with the best source of information in that town: Pepe the janitor (Vladimir Sokoloff). Pepe takes one look at the photos of the body and declares that it's the work of a werewolf. That's crazy of course, but then again he's asking the janitor so what does he expect? A CSI analysis of the bite wounds?

As the police struggle with the case, things carry on almost normally for Tony, who has no memory of the transformation or the attack. Despite being an insane killer werewolf sometimes, Tony's actually doing better in school. He even wins a scholarship! He's so excited that when he hears the school bell ring he turns into his fuzzy self again. This time he murders gymnast Theresa (Dawn Richards) while she's working out alone.

Since werewolf Tony didn't think to take off his school jacket, the whole world now knows that Tony is a teenage werewolf. He heads for Dr. Brandon for help, but let's face it, in the 1950s it was hard enough being a teenager, let alone a teenage werewolf.

The Food

Our hero has a few anger issues, to say the least, but that doesn't mean he fails to provide at least a few food clues during the course of the movie. I'll start by saying that this may be a 1950s teen movie but there will be NO milkshakes drunk while viewing. He makes his feelings quite clear when he throws the bottle of milk against the wall of his kitchen. I get it – no milkshakes!

This scene does provide us with our meal, though. As Dad leaves for work, he mentions the lamb chops in the fridge, with a warning not to eat them raw the same way he did with the hamburger. (Hmmm… could he have had wolfy tendencies even before his regression?) We all know that werewolves are carnivores, so we will dine well tonight on our teenage lamb chops.

Lamb Chops with Garlic

Serves 2

4-6 lamb chops (The size and thickness of the chops will determine if you want to allow for 2 or 3 each.)
Salt and pepper
½ tsp dried thyme
2 tbsp. olive oil
4 cloves garlic, peeled and cut in half
2 tbsp. water
Splash of lemon juice
½ tsp red pepper flakes
1 tbsp. fresh chopped parsley

Sprinkle each lamb chop with some of the salt and pepper, and the thyme. Heat the oil in a skillet over a medium-high heat. Cook the lamb chops and the garlic for 3-4 minutes on either side, until the chops are browned and done to your preference. Remove the chops from the skillet. Do NOT remove the garlic.

Add the water, lemon juice, and red pepper flakes to the pan with the garlic. Cook for about 2 minutes.

Serve the lamb chops on a bed of bean mash (see next recipe) and with the garlic sauce poured on top. Garnish with fresh parsley.

Bean Mash

Serves 2

1 tbsp. olive oil
1 clove garlic, crushed
Zest of 1 lemon
1 can cannellini beans, drained and rinsed (2 if you're extra hungry.)
Salt and pepper

Heat the oil over a medium heat in a pan. Add the garlic and lemon zest and stir for a minute. Add the beans to the pan and warm through, smashing with a spoon as you stir. Season to taste.

If you prefer a smoother puree, add a little more oil and blend with a hand blender.

FROM HELL IT CAME

From Hell It Came (1957)
Directed by Dan Milner
Written by Richard Bernstein and Jack Milner
Produced by Milner Brothers Productions

The Story

> *Fun Facts*
>
> *According to "Watch the Skies" by Bill Warren, Tabonga the tree monster was designed by Paul Blaisdell, the man behind the monsters in The She Creature, It Conquered the World, and Invasion of the Saucermen.*
>
> *In "Leonard Maltin's Movie Guidebook" the film critic gives the movie only 1 & ½ out of 4 stars. However, he does admit that "as walking tree movies go, this one is at the top of the list".*
>
> *The movie poster shows the Tobonga's blood as red, but in the film it is described as green (but it's black and white so we'll take their word for it...*
>
> *Professional wrestler Chester Hayes played Prince Maku and was the actor inside the Tobonga suit.*
>
> *One of only three movies directed by Dan Millner. However, he had a 30 year career as an editor working on cartoons like Popeye The Sailor and television shows like Bozo The Clown.*

There is trouble in paradise for poor Kimo. He's found himself staked to the ground surrounded by chickens. Why chickens? Who knows? What we do know is that he's the son of the late chief of his tribe and the new chief, along with his witch doctor Tano, have accused Kimo of killing his father. They claim the 'white doctor's' medicines Kimo gave him did it. The fact that Tano had been poisoning the chief isn't brought up. Kimo's only hope is the testimony of his wife Kory. Unfortunately, Kory has been doing the hula dance with the new chief and plans to marry him.

Kimo doesn't take this lying down.... Well, he is lying down with chickens around him, but that's beside the point. Just before they stab him in the heart with a ceremonial dagger, he swears he'll rise from the grave and seek vengeance. The natives then bury him vertically in an elaborate coffin made to look like a tree trunk.

The whole scene is witnessed by May Kilgrove, a local widow with a terrible fake British accent. The tribe blames the 'white devils' for the sickness on the island, so when they see her the new chief orders her killed. Since May insists on calling everyone she meets "Ducky" it's possible he just wanted her dead for that. Whatever the case, the natives are after her. She escapes to the lab of Professor Clark and Dr. Arnold, two researchers working on the island to help the locals with the plague that's been killing them. They are also studying the effects of nuclear testing conducted 1500 miles away since a typhoon carried the fall-out to the island.

The doctors are soon joined by another doctor, Terry Mason. Dr. Arnold immediately begins putting the moves on her. The trio of doctors is warned by some of Kimo's friends that they are in danger from the new chief. Of course, they ignore this. Arnold is splitting his time between trying to cure the plague the island is facing and trying to get in Terry's pants. He doesn't seem to be having much luck on either front, so he decides to drive her out to ceremonial burial grounds. They find a strange tree growing on the spot where Kimo was buried. The tree seems to have a heartbeat and the ceremonial dagger used to kill Kimo is embedded in it. The fact that the tree has a crazy scary face and eyes doesn't seem to concern anyone.

Kimo's friends inform the doctors that his spirit has come back to seek revenge in the form of a tree monster called the Tabonga. The witch doctor and new chief plan to enslave it and use it to kill their enemies, including Kory. Hearing this, Kory flees to the doctors for help. They dig up the strange tree before it can be enslaved, not because they believe the story, but because it's radioactive and they want to study it.

The tree monster seems to be dying so Dr. Mason decides to try an experimental heart drug on it. They hook up an IV to its non-existent tree veins and go home because it's a good idea to leave tree monsters unattended.

The drug works and the Tabonga escapes. It goes on a killing spree, shuffling its way across the island waiting for its victims to run into it (which they all seem to do).

The natives dig a pit trap and when the Tabonga shambles into it, they set it on fire. Then, in the time-honored tradition of elaborate death traps by villains, everyone leaves before seeing if it worked. Oddly, the wooden Tabonga appears fireproof and isn't killed. So it climbs out and shuffles on over to kill the chief, the witch doctor and Kory, none of whom seem to be able to avoid the lumbering hunk of angry wood.

All the doctors are now out looking for the creature. Dr. Mason, unable to see the Tabonga for the trees, is grabbed. The other doctors and their assistant open fire and the monster drops her, turning to face them. In doing so, it exposes the dagger in its chest. The doctors think the dagger is the creature's weakness and shoot the handle, driving the blade further into the Tabonga. The monster is apparently killed and sinks in the quicksand. This leaves Dr. Mason free to swoon over Dr. Arnold and the natives free to embrace white medicine and the decline of their own culture.

The Food

For the food, this movie needs a tropical island theme. The chicken is marinated for a long time in the soy sauce mixture, resulting in a very different texture to what one might expect. Add some pineapple and plantains for a South Pacific feel.

And you can't have dessert for this meal without paying homage to the mighty Tabonga. Feel free to get creative with the chocolate bark, making it resemble the movie's tree as closely as you can. Luckily, this is one bark you won't have to run away from. Instead, you'll be running to eat more.

Tropical Chicken Skewers

Serves 2-3

2 chicken breasts, cut into strips
½ small can pineapple chunks in juice, drained
½ cup / 120ml soy sauce
¾ cup / 175ml sesame oil
2 tbsp. white vinegar
3 tbsp. honey
2 cloves garlic, minced
2 tsp ginger
1 tsp red pepper flakes

Pour the soy sauce, sesame oil, vinegar, honey, garlic, ginger, and pepper flakes into a ziplock bag. Add the chicken and leave to marinade for up to a day.

Thread chicken pieces and pineapple chunks on skewers and broil for 5-10 minutes until the meat is cooked.

Plantain Tostones

Serves 2

1 large plantain
2 tbsp. olive oil

Peel the plantain and cut into slices about ½ inch in thickness.

Heat the olive oil in a skillet over medium heat. When hot, add the plantain slices and cook for 3-4 minutes on each side. Remove from the pan and drain on paper towels. Then squash the slices to half of their original thickness. Return the flattened slices to the pan and cook for 3 or 4 more minutes on each side until golden and lightly crisp on the outside.

Serve with the chicken skewers.

Spicy Chocolate Bark

16oz / 450g good quality dark chocolate
12oz / 340g good quality milk chocolate
2 tbsp. ancho chili powder
1 tbsp. chili powder or red pepper flakes
1 tbsp. paprika
1 tbsp. cinnamon
Chunks of dried pineapple, mango, papaya

Line a baking tray with waxed paper.

Melt the dark chocolate in a microwave-safe bowl, stirring every 30 seconds. Stir into the melted chocolate the chili powders, paprika, and cinnamon.

Pour the chocolate onto the baking tray and use a spatula to spread evenly. Sprinkle with chunks of dried fruit.

Place the tray in the fridge to set up for 15-20 minutes to set up.

Melt the milk chocolate in a microwave-safe bowl. When smooth and melted, pour over the first layer of chocolate and dried fruit. Return to the fridge to harden.

Once set, break the chocolate bark into chunks. Store in a tin in a cool place.

20 MILLION MILES TO EARTH

20 Million Miles to Earth (1957)
Directed by Nathan H. Juran (Credited as Nathan Hertz)
Written by Robert "Bob" Creighton Williams and Christopher Knopf (Screenplay) Charlotte Knight (Original Story)
Produced by Morningside Productions

The Story

Fishermen from a small Italian village are surprised by the day's catch: a spaceship!
America's first manned mission to Venus has returned, but things didn't go too well and now the ship has crashed in the Mediterranean. The fishermen board the ship and search for survivors, but are only able to save two men before the ship sinks.

With no doctor available, the villagers contact a zoologist, Dr. Leonardo (Frank Puglia), who's traveling the area collecting specimens of sea life. He isn't able to help, but his granddaughter Marisa (Joan Taylor), one year away from completing her medical degree, agrees to help and is taken to the wounded astronauts.

The two survivors are Colonel Bob Calder (William Hopper) and Dr. Sharman (Arthur Space). Calder is mostly uninjured. However, Sharman dies. Calder, with little regard for any kind of operational security, explains that he and his crew were returning from Venus where most of them had succumbed to a strange illness. The fact that a strange illness from Venus has killed his crew and that he could have brought it to Earth seems to be of no importance and is quickly forgotten. What is important is a sample of life from Venus that he believes scientists can study. Calder assumes the sample is lost.

> ### Fun Facts
>
> *The film is set in Italy, partly because Ray Harryhausen had always wanted to vacation there.*
>
> *This was the last film Ray Harryhausen did in black and white. He'd actually wanted the film to be in color, but the production could not afford it. Harryhausen would later work with colorization company Legend Films to create a color version of the movie in time for the film's 50th anniversary in 2007.*
>
> *The creature in the film was called the Ymir by Harryhausen and the original title of the project was "The Giant Ymir". However, the creature is never referred to as the Ymir in the film because Harryhausen had some concern about audiences confusing the name with the Arabic word emir.*
>
> *Harryhausen determined that the Ymir did not eat meat. When it attacks and kills a dog at a farm it ignores the animal in favor of eating sacks of sulfur kept as fertilizer by the farmer.*

A local boy named Pepe (Bart Bradley) finds a canister with the sample, a large jelly-like egg. Deciding this could be his ticket to the 200 lire he needs to buy a cowboy hat, Pepe takes the specimen to Dr. Leonardo. Leonardo pays him and is delighted when it hatches to reveal a small, humanoid lizard-like creature.

Back in the village, General A.D. McIntosh (Thomas Browne), the head of the Venus mission command, arrives to investigate. He and Calder begin questioning the villagers to see if there is any chance that their sample survived. They offer a large reward, which catches the entrepreneurial ear of Pepe. He tells them what happened and the authorities go to find Dr. Leonardo.

> **Fun Facts**
>
> *Harryhausen's stop-motion animation process was called "Electrolytic Dynamation" in press material for the film.*
>
> *The production called for a real elephant to be used for some scenes. To match the scale of the Ymir, Harryhausen wanted it to be 15ft tall. The best the film could get was an 8ft tall elephant so they cast a short actor, 4'6 to play the zookeeper and help create the feel that the animal was bigger than it was.*

Though only about a day has passed, the creature has grown to man-size and it manages to escape from Leonardo and his granddaughter before the authorities arrive. The Americans convince the Italians to let them try and take the creature alive, even after it kills a local farmer.

Calder tells the team that the creature is growing much faster and larger than they'd seen on Venus and guesses it is due to Earth's atmosphere. He also explains that electricity causes paralysis in the animal so they set a trap and manage to capture the beast.

A team of scientists, including Dr. Leonardo, begin studying the alien in a lab at the Rome zoo. The creature continues to grow and is more than 20 feet tall when it escapes due to an accident cutting the power to its electrified restraints.

The creature smashes its way out of the zoo, battling an elephant in one memorable scene. It then heads out into the city of Rome where it terrorizes the residents until Calder and an Army team chase it into the Colosseum. There, with little regard to the historic setting, the Army proceeds to shoot bazookas at the creature until they chase it up onto the highest edge of the structure. Calder shoots the wall out from under it and the monster falls to its death.

The Food

Since the film is set in Italy, a pasta dish was the obvious choice. But spaghetti and meatballs seemed a little too obvious. Instead, we took our inspiration from a more specific location where much of the movie took place – Sicily. And with all those fishermen, a nice piece of grilled swordfish was the perfect addition to the menu. The result is a meal that's very easy to make and is equally suited to a casual summery lunch or to entertaining friends on the patio with a good bottle of wine.

Tomato Gorgonzola Salad

Serves 2

4 fresh Roma tomatoes (Any fresh tomatoes will do)
½ red onion
½ cup / 50g crumbled Gorgonzola cheese
Fresh basil leaves
Balsamic vinegar
Extra-virgin olive oil
Salt and pepper

Cut the Roma tomatoes into quarters lengthways.
Slice the red onion into rings. You can chop into smaller pieces if you like. (This is a salad so no hard and fast rules).
Put the tomatoes and onions in a salad bowl. Crumble in the Gorgonzola. Throw in some fresh basil leaves. Mix together.
Immediately before serving, drizzle with a little balsamic vinegar and olive oil, and top off with a sprinkling of salt and pepper.

Pasta in Sun-dried Tomato Sauce

Serves 2

We kept this sauce very simple, but it's a great base for experimenting. A lot of recipes add almonds, walnuts, or pine nuts to this, so feel free to try adding your favorites.

1-2 cloves garlic
½ can chopped tomatoes
1/3 cup / 20g sun-dried tomatoes in oil
5 or 6 fresh basil leaves
Red pepper flakes
Salt and pepper
1/3 cup / 35g freshly grated Parmesan
2 ½ cups / 225g penne (or similar) pasta

Cook the pasta to your preference.

Peel the garlic and chop it finely.

Blend together the garlic, tomatoes, sun-dried tomatoes (and their oil), basil, pepper flakes (to your taste), and season with salt and pepper.

Drain the cooked pasta and toss with the sauce. If you prefer a warm sauce, return the pasta to the pan for a minute or two. Alternatively, you can serve as is with the sauce at room temperature. Sprinkle with Parmesan and decorate with additional basil leaves.

Grilled Swordfish Steaks

Serves 2

2 swordfish steaks
3 tbsp. olive oil
½ cup / 25g fresh breadcrumbs
Juice of ½ lemon
1 clove garlic
Handful fresh parsley
1 tbsp. fresh oregano leaves

Brush no more than 1 tbsp. of the olive oil on the fish and sprinkle the steaks with breadcrumbs. The goal is not to cover the fish in a heavy breading, but to provide a light crunch. Grill the swordfish steaks for about 5 minutes on each side, until the crumbs are golden and the fish is cooked.

While the fish is cooking, peel and chop the garlic clove. Combine the remaining olive oil with the lemon juice, garlic, and fresh herbs.

Serve the fish with the herb sauce spooned on top.

SPECIAL EFFECTS FOCUS ON RAY HARRYHAUSEN

"20 Million Miles to Earth" earns a special note because it features the work of Ray Harryhausen. Harryhausen was the mastermind behind some of Hollywood's greatest and most innovative special effects.

Ray Harryhausen celebrating his birthday with a little "Medusa" cake. Original photo courtesy of photographer Mark Mawston.

Harryhausen loved the special effects created by Willis O'Brien for the 1933 hit "King Kong". He was so inspired that he started doing his own stop-motion projects. When a friend introduced him to O'Brien, the effects artist encouraged Harryhausen to take classes in sculpture and graphic design to improve his craft. His big break though came when he later worked with O'Brien on "Mighty Joe Young" in 1947.

"The YMIR" model by Ray Harryhausen with the original lamppost that he bent over in the film. Photo courtesy of Mark Mawston/Ray & Diana Harryhausen Foundation.

Harryhausen was soon creating his own creatures and developing special effects techniques that continue to amaze and inspire filmmakers today. His first solo feature film project was "The

Beast From 20,000 Fathoms" which was a big hit for Warner Brothers. This was quickly followed by "It Came From Beneath the Sea" and "Earth vs The Flying Saucers". The effects master would go on to work on a dozen more features all the way up to 1981's "Clash of the Titans".

We give special mention to Ray Harryhausen here because of the many contributions he made to the science fiction and fantasy film genres and to the film industry as a whole. He inspired generations of filmmakers including: Steven Spielberg, Peter Jackson, John Landis and James Cameron, and his work has delighted audiences for decades. On his 90th birthday the British Academy of Television and Film Arts (BAFTA) presented him with a special award. Today the Ray and Diana Harryhausen foundation works to preserve his legacy for future generations of fans and filmmakers.

Fiona and I are fortunate enough to be friends with photographer Mark Mawston, a friend of the late Harryhausen. Mark contributed many of the poster images seen in our book as well as these photos of Ray and his work.

We are also sharing a recipe for prawn salad. One of Mark's favorite memories of Harryhausen was that each Thursday he would buy some fresh prawns to enjoy. So when you're eatin your prawns think of the man who brought creatures to life and amazed and inspired many of today's greatest filmmakers.

Prawn Salad (a Ray Harryhausen favorite)

This is one of those recipes that some people hate because there are no quantities. Let's face it, a salad is a personal thing. Some people want a ton of lettuce but no red pepper, while others want onions and cucumbers galore. The same for the dressing – make it as minty or spicy as you like. This is just your starting guideline.

Lettuce
Tomatoes, quartered
Cucumber, sliced
Red Pepper, diced
Spring onions, sliced
Fresh prawns

Dressing:
Greek yogurt
Fresh mint
Tabasco
Lemon juice
Black pepper

Mix the mix, lemon juice, black, pepper, and tabasco into the yogurt to suit your taste. I then like to stir the prawns into the dressing. Put a nice generous dollop on top of your lettuce, tomatoes, cucumber, red pepper, spring onions, or other salad accoutrements.

THE BLOB

The Blob (1958)
Directed by Irvin S. Yeaworth Jr. (credited) and Russell S. Doughten (uncredited)
Written by Theodore Simonson and Kay Linaker (writing as Kay Phillips)
Produced by Jack H. Harris and Paramount Pictures

The Story

Teenagers Steve (Steve McQueen) and Jane (Aneta Corsaut) are out at Lover's Lane. A little kissing aside, not much action is going on and Steve decides he'll just buy Jane a sandwich…. Sure why not? Suddenly, the pair sees a meteor fly overhead and crash into the woods not far away.

The meteor lands near an old man's cabin and the old guy does what any sensible person would do -- he starts poking it with a stick. The meteor breaks open and some space snot attaches itself to his stick. That seems pretty interesting until the ooze races up the stick and covers his hand. Steve and Jane almost run over the old guy when he stumbles into the road. They rush him to the town doctor, who doesn't know what to make of the goop that is now covering most of the old guy's arm.

After it finishes eating the old man, the young Blob makes a snack of the nurse. Steve and Jane then see it eat the doctor. They escape to the police station and convince Lt. Dave (Earl Rowe) and Sgt. Bert (John Benson) to check it out. However, the Blob is already gone and there is no evidence of foul play.

The cops think it's a bad joke and send the teens home

> ### Fun Facts
>
> *Twenty-seven-year-old Steve McQueen was paid $2500 to play teenager Steve Andrews. He was offered 10% of the film's profits if he would take a smaller salary upfront, but he opted for the upfront cash, thinking that the film might not do that well. That's too bad because "The Blob" was a hit for Paramount and grossed more than $4 million at the box office.*
>
> *Phoenixville, PA was one of the main filming locations for "The Blob" including the movie theater and diner scenes. Since 2000, the town holds an annual "Blobfest" where fans come and re-enact the scene of the crowd fleeing the movie theater.*
>
> *There were two blobs. In some scenes, a water filled bladder was used. However, most scenes used a silicone gel creation purchased from Union Carbide. Red dye was added to give it color. Producer Jack H. Harris has said that the blob changes color during the film because they added more dye to it each time it ate someone.*

> **Fun Facts**
>
> *The silicone gel blob has never dried out and is featured each year at "Blobfest" along with other props from the film.*
>
> *Steve McQueen is listed as "Steven McQueen" in the film's credits.*
>
> *The film's title song "The Blob" was written by Burt Bacharach and Mack David and became a surprise hit. The song is listed as being performed by "The Five Blobs", which were, in fact, all singer Bernie Nee whose vocals were overdubbed five times.*

with their parents. Being 'trouble makers', Steve and Jane sneak out and gather Steve's friends to help them find the Blob. Meanwhile, the Blob's been out eating mechanics, janitors, and as many folks as it can catch at the local bar. With each person it eats, the Blob grows bigger.

Steve and Jane head to the grocery store, only to find the Blob doing some late night shopping. They manage to escape into the store's walk-in freezer. The Blob starts to come in after them but recoils from the cold. Instead, it lumbers into the local movie theater and makes a snack of the projectionist. It then oozes out into the auditorium; the crowd panics and flees the theater. Now the cops know Steve and Jane aren't lying.

Jane's little brother decides to use his cap guns to shoot the Blob. The teens are able to save him but have to take shelter in a diner. The Blob covers the diner and starts to get in. Steve, Jane, her brother and the diner staff hide in the basement. They spray the Blob with a CO2 fire extinguisher. This freezes part of it and makes it retreat.

Steve is able to let the cops know what will stop the Blob. The teens get all of the extinguishers from the high school. They return and spray the Blob, turning it into a giant frozen custard ready for the army to pick up and drop in the Arctic. We're all saved until global warming's true danger is known!

The Food

Near the beginning of the movie, our hero Steve (played by Steve McQueen) is apologizing to his date, Jane. As part of his apology, he offers to make it up to her with a sandwich. Needless to say, they never get that sandwich, so we will have it for them. But what to put in said sandwich? Luckily, the movie provided inspiration here. Remember that scene where they are hiding in the meat locker at the grocery store? Seeing the meat hanging on hooks and cases of sauerkraut on the shelves, it seems obvious that, had they ever made it to food, Steve would have bought Jane a good old Reuben.

As much as I always had a pink molded blancmange in mind whenever I thought about The

Blob, upon another viewing, it was clear to me that a red jello seemed much more appropriate, given its similarity to a large dollop of raspberry jam. But the flavor for our dessert is influenced by the grocery store in the movie, advertising red ripe watermelons for just 4c.

Reuben with a Kick

Serves 2

4 slices good quality rye bread
8 large slices pastrami
½ cup / 75g sauerkraut
4 large slices Swiss cheese
4 tbsp. butter
Olive oil

Sriracha Russian Dressing:
½ cup / 110 g mayonnaise
2 tbsp. tomato ketchup
1 tbsp. sriracha
1 tbsp. horseradish
1 tsp mustard

Salt and pepper to taste

Mix together all of the dressing ingredients in a small bowl. Add more sriracha or horseradish if you want more of a kick. Put to one side.

In a skillet, drizzle a small amount of olive oil. Now warm the pastrami. We don't want to cook it so much as give it a little warming up. Put on a plate when done.

Heat the sauerkraut in a small pan and keep to one side.

Butter one side of each slice of rye bread. Using the already-warmed skillet that you used for the pastrami, toast the bread, buttered side down.

Keeping the bread in the skillet, put 2 tbsp. of the dressing on a slice of bread. Then pile on the pastrami, sauerkraut, and cheese. Top with another slice of bread. Cook for a minute or two so the cheese starts to melt.

Cut your sandwich in half and serve with a pickle and plenty of napkins

Chocolate Malt

Serves 1-2

1 container good quality vanilla ice-cream
2 – 2 ½ tbsp. chocolate syrup
½ cup / 125 ml whole milk
3 tbs malt powder (such as Ovaltine)
Whipped cream
Maraschino cherry

Put three generous scoops of vanilla ice cream in your blender. Add the chocolate syrup and milk. Finally, sprinkle in the malt powder, and mix until you have a good, thick malted milk. Pour into one or two glasses (depending on if you feel like sharing).
Top with whipped cream and a cherry.

Blob-mange

2 packs watermelon jello
1 cup / 200 ml boiling water
½ lb. / 225g watermelon chunks
½ cup / 125 ml evaporated milk

Puree the watermelon chunks in a blender.

Pour the boiling water over the jello crystals and stir until they've dissolved. Leave to cool for about 10 minutes. Stir in the watermelon puree and the evaporated milk. Pour into mold or keep in bowl and place in the fridge. Leave for several hours until set firm.

ATTACK OF THE 50 FOOT WOMAN

Attack of the 50 Foot Woman (1958)
Directed by Nathan H. Juran (Credited as Nathan Hertz)
Written by Mark Hanna
Produced by Woolner Brothers Pictures, Inc.

The Story

It's hard being rich. Just ask Nancy Archer (Allison Hayes). Her gold digger husband Harry (William Hudson) only married her for her money and was more than happy to check her into a sanitarium when she had a nervous breakdown. Now Nancy is home, but she's got a serious drinking problem and Harry is doing everything he can to encourage the next breakdown so he can get her committed for good, keeping her money and having ready access to his mistress, Honey Parker (Yvette Vickers).

Harry thinks he's found his chance when Nancy staggers into town claiming that her car went off the road out in the desert because an alien spaceship landed. She also claims a giant humanoid alien picked her up and took her back to the ship, but she escaped. Of course, no one believes her. So Nancy tells Harry to take her back to the desert where she saw the ship. If they can't find any evidence of the alien, she'll check back into the sanitarium.

Seeing dollar signs in front of his eyes, Harry agrees. Sure enough, they find the ship and the giant alien. Harry takes a few shots at the alien with his gun, but they have no effect. He runs off, leaving Nancy behind.

Harry figures he's rid of her for sure now, but she turns

> ### Fun Facts
>
> Director Nathan H. Juran won an Academy Award for his work as art director on How Green Was My Valley in 1942 and was nominated for another Academy Award for the 1946 film The Razor's Edge.
>
> Juran directed a number of other science fiction films in the 1950s and 60s including 20 Million Miles to Earth, The Deadly Mantis, and The 7th Voyage of Sinbad.
>
> The movie poster for Attack of the 50 Foot Woman was named #8 in Premiere Magazine's list of the 25 best movie posters ever made.
>
> The film was remade for HBO Pictures in 1993 and starred Daryl Hannah as the 50ft. woman.
>
> Director Jim Wynorski was set to do a remake of the film in the 1980s and even shot some test stills of actress Sybil Danning dressed as the 50ft. woman. He opted to instead direct the remake of another 1950s science fiction film Not of this Earth

up later on the roof of their pool house. She's delirious and Harry has the family doctor (Roy Gordon) sedate her. The doctor thinks that she may have been exposed to some radiation, but doesn't really do much about it.

Harry's mistress Honey convinces him that this is the perfect chance to get rid of Nancy. She urges him to give her an overdose of the sedatives left by the doctor. However, when Harry goes to give her the shot, he finds that she's grown to giant size. He calls the doctor and a specialist, but the best they can do is keep the giant woman sedated and chained up so she won't hurt anyone.

Turning into a giant seems to have caught the attention of the local authorities as the sheriff (George Douglas) and her butler Jess (Ken Terrell) go to investigate. They find the alien, which has been collecting diamonds to power its ship.

> **Fun Facts**
>
> The film was shot in just eight days for a budget of just under $90,000. The film's director Nathan H. Juran is credited by his middle name "Hertz" because he was reportedly embarrassed by the film's low budget and production values.
>
> The film's short 66 minute run time meant that the distributor had to stretch the film to release it on television. This was done with longer than normal opening and closing credit crawls, freezing on some frames and repeated sequences to add another 9 minutes to bring it to 75 minutes for commercial TV.

Meanwhile, Nancy wakes up and decides she's had enough of her cheating husband and his floozy. She puts on a bikini made of bed sheets and heads to town, where she busts through the roof of the local bar and kills Honey. She picks up Harry but the sheriff arrives and tries to stop her. His bullets have no effect though. Instead, he shoots a power line transformer near her and it blows up, killing her. Harry didn't get away though as he's found dead in her hand.

The moral of the story: don't mess with your wife when she's 50 feet tall.

The Food

For a movie about a giant we thought we'd mix it up a little with some mini dishes and something that giant too!

Mini pizzas

Makes about a dozen

1 pack refrigerated pizza dough
½ lb. / 225g ground beef or turkey
½ cup / 125g salsa
¾ cup / 75g shredded cheese

Preheat oven to 200°C/400°F. Line a cookie sheet with parchment paper or spray with nonstick spray.
Roll out the pizza dough and cut into 12 small rounds. Bake for 5 minutes. Remove from oven.

Meanwhile, brown the ground beef or turkey in a skillet. Drain away any fat.
Spoon a little salsa onto each pizza base. Top with cooked ground beef and shredded cheese. Return to the oven until the cheese has melted.

Mini burgers

Makes 12

1 pack mini burger buns
1 lb. / 450g ground beef
¾ cup / 75g shredded cheese
Burger toppings – mustard, ketchup, relish, etc.

Preheat oven broiler. Split the buns in half. You can toast them or use them as is.
Divide the meat into 12 equal portions and shape into mini patties. Place the patties on a baking sheet and broil for 10 minutes. Sprinkle shredded cheese on each patty and return the sheet to the broiler for a few more minutes until the cheese is melted.
Place a patty in each bun and serve with your favorite burger accompaniments.

Rice Salad

Again, no quantities here because you make it to suit the number of people you are feeding.

Enough cooked rice for the number of people being served
Chopped red onion
Cooked peas
Chopped red pepper
Sliced almonds (optional)
Mayonnaise
Sriracha or other favorite chili sauce
Salt and pepper

Stir the onion, peas, red pepper and almonds into the rice.
Mix the mayonnaise and sriracha to your preferred level of heat, and then stir into the rice mix.
Season with salt and pepper.

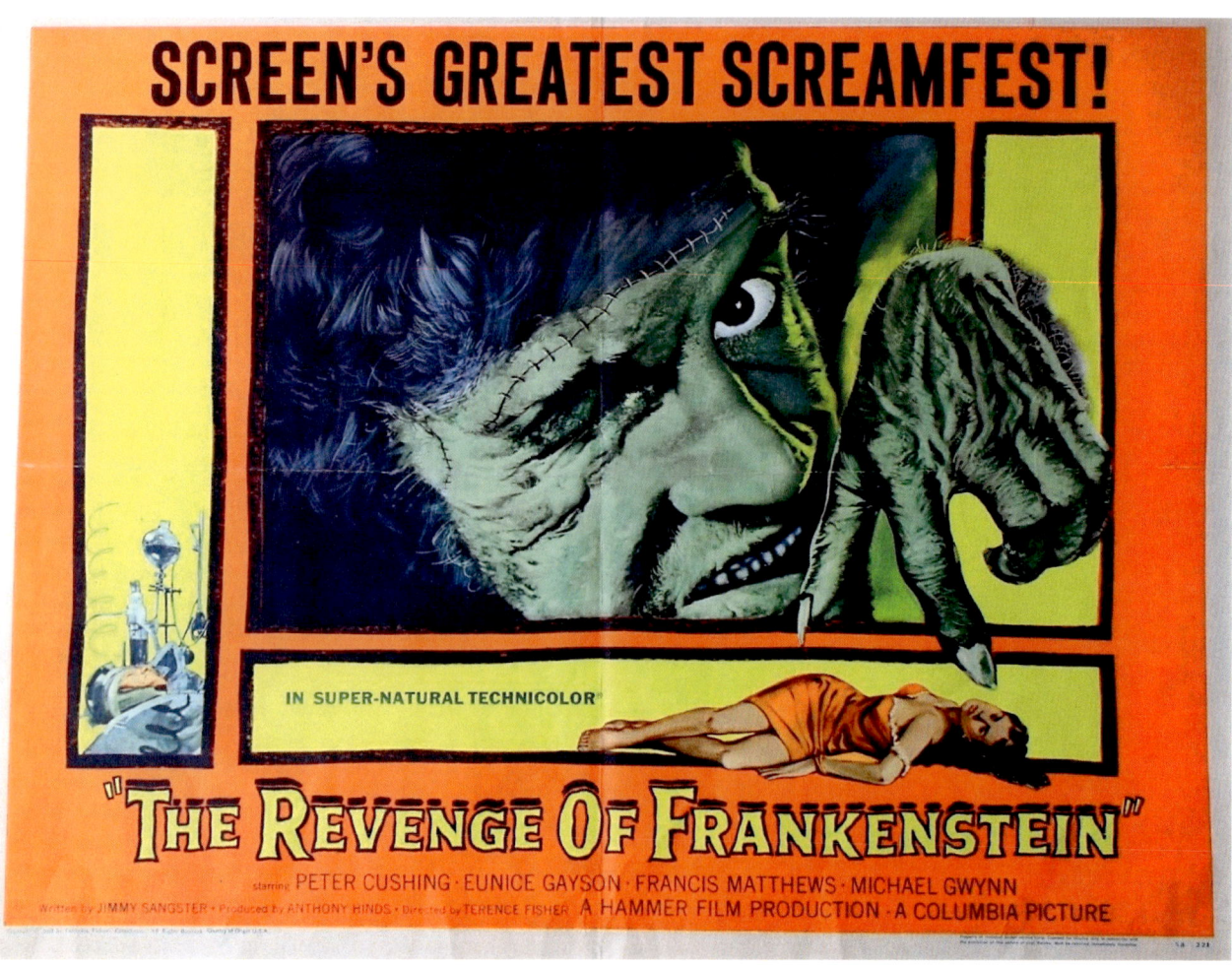

THE REVENGE OF FRANKENSTEIN

The Revenge of Frankenstein (1958)
Directed by Terence Fisher
Written by Jimmy Sangster
Produced by Hammer Studios

The Story

> ### Fun Facts
>
> *Writer Jimmy Sangster started work for Hammer Studios as a production manager.*
>
> *Sangster wrote a number of Hammer Horror films including many of their re-imaginings of the Universal Horror films: The Curse of Frankenstein, Dracula (renamed Horror of Dracula in the U.S. to avoid confusion with the 1931 film) and The Mummy.*
>
> *The film's director, Terence Fisher, was also a staple of Hammer Horror films. He directed many of the films Sangster penned including all of the ones listed above.*
>
> *The film was shot back-to-back with Hammer's Dracula, so many of the sets were used in both films. Peter Cushing was also in both movies.*

Baron Victor Frankenstein (Peter Cushing) is facing execution after the events of The Curse of Frankenstein (1957), and it looks like the end as he's marched to the guillotine. However, Frankenstein is not that easy to kill. His hunchbacked assistant Karl (Oscar Quitak) helps him escape, substituting the priest who has come to read the last rites in his place.

Years later Frankenstein, re-invented as Dr. Stein, has taken up residence in Carlsbruck. He's started a very successful practice there, much to the ire of the town's medical council. It seems many of the town's richest citizens have been giving their business to Dr. Stein. It also doesn't help that he's popular with the poor folks too, thanks to a free clinic he works at.

Things are going well for the doctor and his experiments continue in secret, until Dr. Hans Kleve (Francis Matthews) recognizes Dr. Stein and blackmails him. Kleve doesn't want money. He wants to study with Frankenstein and help with his experiments. Frankenstein agrees and the duo begins working together. Karl the hunchback is excited too because Frankenstein has promised that Karl will be the first patient to have his brain transplanted into a new body. Karl imagines that once he's in a new body he'll have a shot at Margaret (Eunice Gayson) the lovely assistant at the hospital.

The operation is a success and Karl gets a new body that looks much better than his old one. Kleve is a little concerned by the fact that during their testing of the process a chimpanzee who had an orangutan's brain placed in it went crazy and ate its mate. But Dr. Stein has no time for trivial side-effects like cannibalism and violent insanity. He has plans to show off the new Karl as his prize exhibit at all the medical universities. New Karl isn't too happy about the prospect of being on display and wants to get away. Stein and Kleve make sure he can't by tying him down, for his own safety of course. Still, Karl's no dummy. He convinces Margaret to loosen his bonds and he escapes.

Karl hides in Stein's lab, where he finds his old body. He burns the body, but before he can escape the janitor comes in and attacks Karl. Karl strangles the man and flees. Margaret finds him hiding in her aunt's barn and tries to help by getting Dr. Kleve, but Karl runs away again. He's having trouble with his arm and leg and is growing ever more crazed as his new body takes on the deformities of his old one. After strangling a young woman, he exposes the Stein's true identity at a reception while begging the doctor to fix him

Stein denies that he's Frankenstein, but the other doctors aren't convinced. They arrange for Frankenstein's grave to be exhumed. There, they discover the body of the priest.

Meanwhile, Dr. Stein tries to seek refuge at his free clinic. No luck. The patients, showing a truly ungrateful nature to the man who'd helped them so much, attack him. Kleve finds Frankenstein near death and rushes him to the lab. Frankenstein had, conveniently enough, been building himself a new body. Karl scoops Frankenstein's brain out and puts it in the new body just in time to present the old body, minus a brain, to the authorities, thus proving Frankenstein is truly dead.

Frankenstein's new body looks a lot like his old one and, unlike his previous attempts, this one seems to work. So Dr. Kleve and the renamed Dr. Franck move to London to start a new practice, and perform more experiments. This is good because Hammer makes five more Frankenstein movies after this one and it's hard to do that with a dead doctor!

The Food

Perfect Roast Chicken

Serves 4

1 3-4 lb. / 1.5-2 kg free-range chicken
2 tbsp. butter
Salt and pepper
Sprigs of fresh herbs of your choosing
½ lemon

Preheat oven to 220°C/425°F.

Wash the chicken and pat dry. Give a good sprinkling of salt and pepper both on the outside of the chicken and in the cavity. Make a few tiny slits in the skin and slot some of the herb sprigs between the skin and the meat. Place the rest of the herbs and the lemon half in the cavity.

Rub the butter onto the skin of the chicken.

Place in a roasting tin and roast for about 1 ½ hours. When the chicken is done, the skin will be golden and crisp, and if you poke a knife into the thickest part of the thigh, the juices will be clear.

Leave the chicken to rest for 10 minutes before carving.

Cushing's Vegetarian Special

Serves 4-6

4-6 beets, washed and peeled
2 sticks celery
2 onions
2 large potatoes, peeled
2 tbsp. olive oil
Salt and pepper

Chop the potatoes into chunks and boil for 10 minutes. Drain.

Slice the celery. Chop the beets and onions into chunks; the beets should be no bigger than a ½ inch for them to cook properly.

Heat the oil in a skillet and sauté the onions for a few minutes until they start to brown. Add the beets and celery and cook for 2 minutes. Lastly, add the potatoes and season with salt and pepper.

Turn the heat to low and cover the skillet. Continue to cook until the potatoes and beets are tender, about 15-20 minutes.

Serve as a side dish or on its own. Alternatively, cover with shredded cheese and place under the grill until the cheese is melted and bubbly.

"It is surprising how my passion for this delicacy will not be taken seriously. Place 1-2 slices (according to appetite) of brown bread under a grill set 'high'. When flames appear, it is done. Reverse until the other side cries for mercy. Do not scrape off the cinders. Served with butter and your favourite marmalade, plus a pot of Indian tea, it constitutes a meal that can be eaten any time of the day or night, and often is by Peter Cushing."

From the book "The Cook Book of the Stars" - Copyright 1983

TEENAGERS FROM OUTER SPACE

Teenagers From Outer Space (1959)
Directed by Tom Graeff
Written by Tom Graeff
Produced by Tom Graeff Productions

The Story

An alien race needs a place to grow their Gargons (giant lobster monsters) for food. Earth looks like a good place so they land their spaceship just outside a small town. One of the aliens, Thor (Bryan Grant) pops out of the spaceship and uses his disintegrator ray on a little dog named Sparky, reducing him to a pile of bones.

Another crew member, Derek (David Love) examines the remains and finds the collar. He argues that the collar means the planet has intelligent life and should be left alone. Thor, the ship's Captain (King Moody), and the rest of the crew mock Derek for being soft. Since their people gave up on romantic and familial love long ago, they see it as a weakness.

Derek demands they leave but when that doesn't work, he flees. Thor is about to shoot him when the Captain stops him, telling him that Derek is actually their Supreme Leader's kid and that Thor needs to go get him while the Captain retrieves the rest of the fleet.

Fun Facts

The futuristic space ray guns used by Thor and Derek were actually dime story "Atomic Disintegrator" guns made by Hubley Toys.

To create the flashing effect of the ray gun firing, a mirror was mounted on the end of the gun and light was then reflected into the film camera.

Whenever the ray guns were used to kill someone in the film, the only thing left would be the victim's bones. To create this effect, filmmaker Graeff used a medical school skeleton. The same one is used for all the victims and at times during the film, the plate used to hang the skeleton for display is clearly visible.

The film was shot almost entirely in and around central Hollywood with numerous landmark buildings in the background. However, Graeff (who also did the cinematography on the film) was still able to create the feeling of a small town through clever camera work to avoid skyscrapers and taller buildings.

Derek wanders into town and tracks down the address from Sparky's collar. The dog was owned by Betty Morgan (Dawn Anderson) and her Grandpa Joe (Harvey B. Dunn). Forgetting the dog, they decide that

unemployed strangers make for great tenants and offer to rent him a room in their house.

Meanwhile, Thor hitches a ride into town and starts vaporizing anyone he finds annoying. Derek, Betty and her boyfriend Joe (played by writer/director Tom Graeff) a reporter, learn that Thor is out there and spend the rest of the afternoon alternatively being chased by and chasing the homicidal alien.

Wounded by the police, Thor kidnaps Betty and Derek to get treated. Several low-speed car chases later and Thor wrecks his car allowing Betty and Derek to escape. Only now Thor is not the problem; the one Gargon that the aliens left behind has turned into a giant, house-size lobster bent on destroying everything in town. With Betty's help, Derek destroys the Gargon.

> ### Fun Facts
>
> *Graeff (a UCLA Film School graduate) posed as a UCLA student working on a film project to get an elderly woman to let him use her home as one of the sets for the film.*
>
> *For several scenes director Graeff had the actors pre-record their dialogue and then lip-sync the dialogue when they acted the scenes out for the camera. Normally, if a scene's dialogue needs to be dubbed it is done after the scene is shot and the actors match their voices to the lip movements.*
>
> *Stress from the production and financing of the film took its toll on Graeff and he had a nervous breakdown in late 1959. He decided he was the second coming of Jesus Christ and was arrested for disrupting a church service.*

Derek leaves Betty and goes to the Supreme Leader, convincing him that he wants to guide the invasion fleet down for a landing. Not seeing a problem, they give Derek control and he crashes the entire fleet into the landing field. This is the end of Derek and the invasion. Derek's ghost head looks creepily down on Earth declaring that he "will make the Earth my home and never, never leave it". Nothing weird about that at all.

The Food

Retro Salmon Mousse

1 tbs unflavored gelatin
3 tbsp. cold water
6 tbsp. boiling water
½ cup / 110g mayonnaise
2 tbsp. lemon juice
1 small shallot, finely chopped
2 drops hot sauce

1 tsp paprika
1 tsp salt
1 large can salmon, drained and flaked
2 tbsp. capers
1 cup / 225 ml whipped cream

If using a mold, grease the inside lightly with butter or cooking spray. Alternatively, you can leave it to set in small ramekins.

Sprinkle the gelatin in the cold water, and then add the boiling water, stirring until the gelatin has dissolved. Add the mayonnaise, lemon juice, shallot, hot sauce, paprika, and salt. Carefully fold in the salmon and capers, followed by the whipped cream. Mix everything together well.

Pour into the mold or ramekins and cover with a layer of saran wrap. Refrigerate overnight.

To unmold, place in a shallow dish of warm water for a few seconds to help loosen up.

Sprinkle with a little more paprika and serve with crackers and crudités.

Stained Glass Cream Pie

Note that the filling makes enough for two pies or one large cake.

To make 1 pie (with leftover filling):

1 package ladyfingers
3 packs of jello in the flavors of your choosing. I used lime, orange, and raspberry.
4 cups / 940 ml boiling water
1½ cups / 350 ml cold water
1 pack lemon jello
¼ cup / 55g sugar
½ cup / 100 ml pineapple juice
2 cups / 450 ml heavy whipping cream

Using one cup of boiling water and ½ cup cold water per pack, make up the three packs of jello, leaving each to set until firm in a square pan. When set, remove from the pans and cut into cubes.

Use the ladyfingers to line the bottom and sides of a pie pan or a spring form cake tin.

Dissolve the lemon jello and sugar in 1 cup of boiling water. Stir in the pineapple juice and place in the fridge for 5-10 minutes until the mixture has started to thicken but is not set.

Whip the cream until thick. Blend the lemon mix into the cream. Lastly, use a spatula to carefully stir in the jello cubes.

Pour into the lined pan and leave to set for at least 5 hours.

HOUSE ON HAUNTED HILL

House on Haunted Hill (1959)
Directed by William Castle
Written by Robb White
Produced by Robb White and William Castle Productions

The Story

Millionaire Fredrick Loren (Vincent Price) likes to throw a party. But he won't settle for appetizers and booze. When he's throwing one for 4th wife Annabelle (Carol Ohmart) he rents a haunted house and invites five seemingly random people to spend the night. Whoever stays the whole night will receive $10,000.

The guests are a varied lot: newspaper columnist Ruth Bridges (Judy Mitchum), psychiatrist David Trent (Alan Marshal), test pilot Lance Schroeder (Richard Long), Watson Pritchard (Elisha Cook) the owner of the house, and Nora Manning (Carolyn Craig) an employee at one of Loren's many companies.

The party doesn't seem to be going well as Annabelle and Loren appear to hate each other. She spends her time drinking and casually telling everyone who'll listen that she expects to die a mysterious death like Loren's last three wives. To add to the fun, Pritchard splits his time between telling everyone that he doesn't approve of Loren having a party in his house and explaining how the house is filled with restless spirits. He also shows everyone the basement which contains a large vat of acid built into the floor, because isn't that a selling feature for any home?

Not to be outdone by all this, Loren gives his guests a little present to make them feel safer -- a

> *Fun Facts*
>
> Director/Producer and consummate showman William Castle used many gimmicks to help promote his films in theaters. For this one Castle released the film in "Emergo". In some participating theaters, a system of wires was set up. At certain points in the film, a plastic skeleton flew over the audience.
>
> Young theater-goers quickly caught on to this gimmick and many times the skeleton would be pelted with rocks and even shot at with slingshots to try and bring it down during the show.
>
> The film was a hit for William Castle's production company, costing about $200,000 to make and grossing over $1,000,000 during its release.

> **Fun Facts**
>
> *Alfred Hitchcock reportedly took notice of Haunted Hill's financial success and decided to make his own low-budget horror film: "Psycho"*
>
> *In the movie posters and lobby cards for the film, the house's exterior appears to be a traditional haunted mansion. In the film, however, the exterior of the house was the Frank Lloyd Wright-designed Ennis house in Los Angeles, CA.*
>
> *The owners of the film's copyright failed to renew it and the movie became a public domain feature, meaning anyone can copy and commercially release the film. This has resulted in numerous low-quality DVD and VHS releases of the film.*

small coffin. Inside each is a .38 caliber pistol. Annabelle doesn't need hers though because she decides the party is a drag and hangs herself. This freaks out the guests, but they're all locked in for the night so they can't leave (which means they automatically win the money unless they join Annabelle).

Nora is upset by Annabelle's death. Lance is upset that he hasn't scored with Nora yet, and Dr. Trent is excited to spend the evening telling Nora she's going crazy with hysteria. Nora thinks he may be right. She sees the ghost of Annabelle outside her window and is attacked by the rope Annabelle hung herself with.

It turns out that Annabelle isn't really dead. She and Dr. Trent are working together to freak out Nora and make her think Loren is a killer. They hope to drive the young woman to shoot him in a fit of panic. They succeed. Trent goes to do the 'plop, plop, fizz, fizz' with Loren's body into the vat of acid, but the lights go out and Trent ends up being the one turned into a skeleton.

Now the rest of the guests must figure out who's really dead, who's really alive and most importantly of all, why Watson Pritchard rented Loren the house in the first place.

The Food

Steak in Red Wine (adapted from A Treasury of Great Recipes by Mary and Vincent Price)

Serves 2

2 steaks
2½ tbsp. butter
1 shallot, finely chopped
1 tsp flour
½ cup red wine

To cook the steaks: Heat 1 tbsp. butter in a skillet over a high heat. Add the steaks and cook for about 4 minutes on each side. Remove steaks from pan and keep warm until ready to serve.

To make the sauce: To skillet that you used for the steaks, add the chopped shallot and ½ tbsp. butter. Cook for about 30 seconds. Add the red wine and continue cooking until the wine has reduced by half.

Mix 1 tsp flour with ½ tbsp. butter until you have a paste. Add this to the wine sauce and cook for 30 seconds. Swirl in the remaining butter just before serving.

Serve the steaks with a little of the sauce spooned on top.

Green Beans with Almonds

Serves 2

2 cups / 225g French green beans (haricots verts)
2 tbsp. sliced almonds
1 tbsp. butter
1 shallot, finely chopped
Salt and pepper
1 tsp lemon zest
1 tsp lemon juice

Trim the tops and tails off the beans.

Toast the almonds in a skillet over a medium-high heat for about 3 minutes, until they are golden.

Bring a pot of salted water to the boil, and blanch the beans for 3 minutes. Drain and rinse in cold water to stop them cooking any further. Dry the beans with a tea towel.

Melt the butter in and add the shallot. Cook for 305 minutes until it starts to brown. Add the beans to the pan, along with the lemon zest and juice. You only want to heat the beans, not cook them too much, so 2 minutes should be plenty.

Remove from the heat, season with salt and pepper and toss with the almonds.

Vincent's Bloody Bet Cocktail

2 parts champagne
1 part blood orange liqueur

Serve in a champagne flute.
Perfect when accompanied by little chocolate coffins.

PLAN 9 FROM OUTER SPACE

Plan 9 From Outer Space (1959)
Directed by Ed Wood
Written by Ed Wood
Produced by Reynolds Pictures, Inc.

The Story

Director Ed Wood, known for his ultra-cheesy films, pulled out all the stops when he wrote and directed "Plan 9 From Outer Space". The film starts with a funeral; an old man (Bela Lugosi) is mourning the passing of his wife. Elsewhere an airliner is heading for Burbank. The pilot, Jeff Trent (Gregory Walcott) and his co-pilot Danny (David De Mering) are shocked at the sight of a plastic model of a flying saucer being dangled in front of the camera… er… I mean by the sight of a flying saucer outside their plane. The pair watches the saucer land in the same graveyard where the old man's wife is being buried.

Shortly after the flying saucer lands, a female ghoul (Vampira) comes out of the woods and kills two grave diggers. Meanwhile, the old man is so lost in his grief that he steps out in front of a car and is killed. This was good for Ed Wood because Bela Lugosi actually died prior to the start of filming. (See trivia sidebar).

Jeff the pilot tells his wife, Paula (Mona McKinnon), about the UFO and how the army has sworn him to secrecy about what he saw, despite the fact that saucers are regularly flying over Hollywood Boulevard. Jeff and his wife hear the sounds of sirens as police come to investigate the death of the grave diggers in the cemetery,

---

Fun Facts

Originally titled "Grave Robbers From Outer Space" the title was reportedly changed because producer J. Edward Reynolds, the leader of the Southern Baptist Convention in Beverly Hills, thought "Grave Robbers" sounded sacrilegious.

In 1956 Bela Lugosi had been working with his friend, director Ed Wood, on a project that was variously titled "Tomb of the Vampire" or "The Ghoul Goes West". They shot footage of Lugosi in his cape walking in a field, attending a funeral and walking in front of a house. When Lugosi died of a heart attack that year, Wood decided to use the footage in "Plan 9" as a tribute to his friend and to get a name actor attached to the project.

Journalist R. H. Greene was able to confirm in 2014 that Vampira (Maila Nurmi) was the model for Maleficent, the evil witch in the Disney's animated "Sleeping Beauty."

which is located conveniently next to their property.

Police Inspector Clay (Tor Johnson) and some other officers wander around the graveyard trying not to knock over the flimsy looking tombstones as they search for clues. Keeping with good horror movie tradition, Inspector Clay decides to go off on his own after everyone is knocked off their feet by the swoosh of a landing flying saucer.

The alien invaders unleash the female ghoul and the now re-animated, and significantly different-looking, old man who both proceed to kill the inspector. Then the aliens pack up and head back to their nearby space station so Alien Commander Eros (Dudley Manlove) and his assistant Tanna (Joanna Lee) can report to their Ruler (John Breckinridge). They tell him that they have been unsuccessful in making contact with Earth's leaders. Since landing and actually talking to someone won't do it for these guys, the aliens decide to enact "Plan 9" which involves reanimating the dead. This will surely get the authorities to listen to their intergalactic plea that the humans stop their destructive behavior before they make a weapon that will cause the sunshine to explode and thereby destroy the entire universe.

> ## Fun Facts
>
> *Ed Wood Jr. often used stock footage to 'beef up' his films. In Plan 9 this included the scenes of the military shooting at the flying saucers.*
>
> *Actress Maila Nurmi (Vampira) was one of the original late night horror hosts working for Channel 7 in Los Angeles. She was nominated for an Emmy Award as "Most Outstanding Female Personality" in 1954.*
>
> *Maila Nurmi appeared in a number of films other than Plan 9 including "Sex Kittens Go To College", "The Beat Generation" and "The Big Operator". In many of her films she was credited as Vampira.*
>
> *Nurmi sued actress Cassandra Peterson claiming that Peterson's "Elvira" character was a direct rip-off of her "Vampira". Despite the similarities, Nurmi lost the lawsuit.*

The aliens reanimate detective Clay and use him and their other ghouls to chase Paula. (Remember her? You know, the Pilot's wife.) After ineffectively menacing her, the aliens lure Trent and some of the police onto their saucer so they can tell them how stupid they are. A fight breaks out and some of the saucer's delicate, cardboard-based systems are damaged. Eros and Tanna fly off only to have their ship explode, leaving the Earth free to continue its Soloronite research so humans can learn to blow up the sunshine and destroy the universe.

The Food

Cheese Straws

Makes 2-3 dozen

2 cups / 250g all-purpose flour
2 cups / 200g grated Cheddar or other strongly flavored cheese
¾ cup / 170g butter
1 tsp baking powder
½ tsp cayenne pepper
½ tsp salt
½ cup / 90ml water

Preheat the oven to 200°C/400°F. Line a baking sheet with parchment paper.

Mix the flour, cheese, butter, baking powder, cayenne pepper, and salt. Add a little water at a time, mixing until you have a stiff dough.
On a floured surface, roll out the dough to about a ¼ inch thickness. Cut into lengths. Either place flat

onto the baking sheet or twirl to form cheese twists.

Bake for 7-10 minutes, until they are golden.

Bacon-topped Cheese Dip

4 slices bacon
2 ¼ cups / 225 g mozzarella, shredded
2 ¼ cups / 225g provolone, shredded
1 cup / 225g cream cheese, room temperature
½ cup / 50g Parmesan
½ cup / 90g roasted red pepper, chopped
1 spring onion, chopped

Cook the bacon until crisp. Preheat oven to 230°C/450°F.

Mix the mozzarella, provolone, cream cheese, and parmesan in an ovenproof dish. Bake for 10-15 minutes until melted and bubbly.

Sprinkle the bacon, red pepper, and onion on top and return to oven for 2 minutes to warm through.

Serve with crackers or cheese straws.

Baked Mac and Cheese Bites

Makes about 30 mini-bites

2 cups / 125g macaroni
2 tbsp. butter
3 tbsp. all-purpose flour
¾ cup / 190ml milk
2 ¼ cups / 225g cheddar cheese, grated

1 tbsp. cream cheese
½ tsp salt
½ tsp pepper
1 egg, beaten
1 tsp cayenne pepper (optional but recommended if you want an extra kick to your bites)
1 tsp smoked paprika

Cook the macaroni in boiling water for 6-8 minutes until al dente, then drain.

Preheat your oven to 200°C/400°F. Grease two mini muffin tins.

Whisk together the butter and flour over a medium heat. Gradually pour in the milk and cook for about 10 minutes until it starts to thicken. Stir in the cream cheese and 200g of the cheese. Season to taste with the salt and pepper. Continue to stir until the sauce is smooth and the cheese has all melted. Remove from the heat.

After allowing the cheese sauce to cool for a few minutes, add the macaroni, beaten egg, and cayenne pepper.

Divide the macaroni mix between the greased muffin tins. Sprinkle with the remaining cheese and the paprika.

Bake for 15 minutes until golden. Remove the trays from the oven and carefully flip the bites over. Bake for 10 more minutes.

Serve warm with your favorite sauce. Barbecue works well, as does a spicy tomato ketchup.

Cheesy Saucer Spamwiches

Sliced white bread
Processed cheese slices
Spam

Cut the bread, cheese, and spam into rounds. Layer the cheese and spam between the bread for the ultimate cheap and cheesy food tribute.

Sugar Cookies

Makes 2-3 dozen cookies

1 cup / 225g unsalted butter, softened
¼ cup / 55g cream cheese, softened
1 cup / 225 g sugar
1 large egg
1 tsp vanilla extract
1 tsp lemon zest
3 cups / 375g flour
1 ½ tsp baking powder

Using a mixer, cream together the softened butter, cream cheese, and sugar. When fluffy, add the egg, vanilla extract, and lemon zest, and mix well.

In a separate bowl, combine the flour and baking powder. Gradually beat into the butter mix to form a soft dough.

Roll the dough in plastic wrap and chill it in the refrigerator for an hour. (Longer is ok).

Preheat oven to 180°C/350°F. When the dough is chilled, remove from the refrigerator and roll out to about ¼ inch thickness. Cut into the shapes you prefer -- we used headstones, coffins, and bats to fit the movie theme. Place the shapes carefully on a baking sheet that has been lined with parchment paper.

Bake the cookies for 8-12 minutes. After removing from the oven, leave on the tray for 5 minutes, before moving to a wire rack. Allow the cookies to cool completely before decorating to your preference.

PHOTO CREDITS

The following movie poster images were provided from the collection of photographer Mark Mawston: 20 Million Miles To Earth, Attack of the 50 Ft. Woman, The Creature From the Black Lagoon (English & French versions), The Blob, It Conquered The World, The Revenge of Frankenstein, I Was A Teenage Werewolf, Them, The Thing From Another World (English & French versions), and Plan 9 From Outer Space

The photo of Ray Harryhausen on his birthday courtesy of Mark Mawston. The photo of the model of the Ymir and the original broken lamppost from 20 Million to Earth courtesy of Mark Mawston and the Ray and Diana Harryhausen Foundation. Neither of these photos may be used or reproduced without express written permission from Mr. Mawston and the Ray and Diana Harryhausen Foundation.

All photos of food were taken by Fiona Young-Brown or Nic Brown and may not be used or reproduced without our express written permission.

Index

Ants in a Tree	39
Bacon-topped Cheese Dip	114
Baked Mac and Cheese Bites	115
Bean Mash	61
Blob-mange	85
Bourbon Nut Brownies	47
Brigadeiros	27
Carrot Cake	20
Cheese Straws	113
Cheesy Saucer Spamwiches	116
Chocolate Irish Cream Cheesecake	45
Chocolate Malt	85
Choco-Rum Mousse	48
Cushing's Vegetarian Special	97
Deconstructed Baked Alaska	19
Garlic Sautéed Mushrooms	53
Green Beans with Almonds	109
Grilled Swordfish Steaks	75
Lamb Chops with Garlic	60
Layered Buttercream Cake	40
Marshmallow Cones	55
Mini burgers	91
Mini pizzas	90
Pasta in Sun-dried Tomato Sauce	74
Perfect Roast Chicken	95
Plantain Tostones	67
Prawn Salad	78
Raspberry Sauce	21
Raymond Burr Roll	34
Retro Salmon Mousse	101
Reuben with a Kick	83
Rice Salad	91
Salmon with Spicy Roast Carrots and Yogurt	15
Scotty's Blueberry Muffins	17
Spicy Chocolate Bark	67
Squid Ink Risotto	26
Stained Glass Cream Pie	102
Steak in Red Wine	107
Sugar Cookies	117
Sushi Rice	33
Sushi rolls	34
Tomato Gorgonzola Salad	72
Tropical Chicken Skewers	66
Vanilla Buttercream	41
Vincent's Bloody Bet Cocktail	109
Yogurt Dill Sauce	54

ABOUT THE AUTHOR

Fiona Young-Brown and Nic Brown met while they were both teaching English in Japan. Fiona introduced Nic to British culture and a taste for international foods. Nic made her watch "Manos: The Hands of Fate". It may not have been a match made in heaven, but it works for them!

When she's not watching B-Movies with Nic, Fiona works as a professional author and freelance writer. Among her works are: *A Culinary History of Kentucky, Wicked Lexington, Nuclear Fusion and Fission (Great Discoveries in Science)* and *The Universe to Scale: Similarities and Differences in Objects in Our Solar System.*

When he's not busy co-hosting the B-Movie Cast, Nic works as a project manager for an international trading company to pay some of the bills. However, his real passions are movies and writing. He's written two novels in his *Werewolf for Hire* series: *Blood Curse and Blood Sacrifice* and has been producing independent films including "Loss Prevention" and "Wretch".

Fiona can be found on the web at www.BritishFoodandTravel.com and Nic can be found at www.BMovieMan.com

Follow them on Twitter:
@FionaYoungBrown
@BMovieMan

Made in the USA
Lexington, KY
29 November 2017